WOODALL'S®

Everywhere RVers Go.

Camping and RVing with

DOGS

The Complete Reference for Dog-Loving Campers and RVers

Jack and Julee Meltzer

WOODALL'S®

Everywhere RVers Go.

Author: Julee & Jack Meltzer
Vice President & Publisher: Ann Emerson
Director of Marketing: Elizabeth Shura
Internet Marketing Manager: Donna Brown
Senior Director of Production: Christine Bucher
Edited by: Brittny Jensen and Annette Ruiz @ AC Services
Proofreader: Tanya Paz and Princesa Rodriguez
Design and Layout: Marsh Media, Ltd.
Cover Camping Photo: Courtesy of GoRVing
Photography: Julee Meltzer

Printed and bound in the United States by Delta Printers.

UPC: 6 15535 92195 3
ISBN: 978-0-7627-5461-8

Other publications available from Woodall's:
Woodall's Campground Directories
Woodall's North American Atlas
Woodall's Cooking on the Road with Celebrity Chefs
Woodall's Campsite Cookbook
Woodall's RV Buyers Guide
Woodall's Camping Life Magazine

For more information about Woodall's products and services go to:
www.woodalls.com or call **1-800-323-9076**

Table of Contents

CHAPTER 4:

Chapter 5:

Chapter 6:

Chapter 7:

Chapter 8:

Chapter 9:
HANDLING MEDICAL PROBLEMS

Introduction

Lilac, a nine year old German Shepherd dog,
has been a full-time RVer for five years.

Like most Northern New Englanders, we have spent much
of our life fighting the cold, shoveling snow, and waiting for
spring. But in 2004, after a particularly severe winter, we
made the decision to change the way we lived. One way or
another – we were going to find a way to spend our winters
in some place warm and sunny. As it happened, the solution
was pretty simple. All we had to do was change our careers,
sell all our belongings, purchase a motorhome, and drive
off. So in September of 2004, we implemented our plan and
headed west with our three cats and two dogs.

Of course as novice full-time RVers, we were anxious to
learn how other RVers with pets handled the day-to-day
challenges of life on the road. How would we deal with
roadside problems or medical emergencies? Would our
dogs be able to adapt to our nomadic lifestyle? Would they

be a problem at crowded campgrounds? Would there be an adequate amount of living space for two adults and two large dogs? We had dozens of questions like these that we wanted to resolve before we headed out. However, when we tried to find useful information about camping and RVing with dogs, we constantly came up empty. Determined to learn all we could about our newly elected lifestyle, we jumped headfirst into the curious but undocumented world of camping and RVing with dogs.

With our two dogs (and three cats), we traveled across the U.S. while staying at a seemingly endless variety of parks, resorts, campgrounds, parking lots, public lands, and neighborhood back streets. In the meantime, we searched the Internet for practical advice and participated in a vast assortment of online forums for campers and RVers who traveled with pets. We took part in campground dog shows, campground dog hikes, dog play groups, and first-aid seminars for people with dogs. We also spoke with park rangers, law enforcement officials, campground owners, animal control professionals, veterinarians, and other campers and RVers (with and without dogs). When we finally gathered a sufficient amount of useful information – we began to write this book.

As you might expect, many people go camping and RVing in America. In fact, RV industry data indicates that more than 8 million U.S. households routinely go camping and RVing each year. Of this number, it has been estimated that nearly half bring their dogs with them. With dog kennels costing anywhere from $20 to $50 a day, RVs offer the perfect way to eliminate the stress and expense of boarding.

This third edition of Camping and RVing with Dogs now represents the most comprehensive collection of essential information for the growing community of campers, RVers, and their canine companions. Like the previous editions, this book reveals the best practices of life on the road along with the unspoken rules of modern campground living.

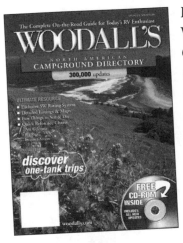

It's also designed to accompany Woodall's North American Campground Directory – the most complete and reliable source of campground, RV service center, and area attraction information. The Directory is annually updated by Woodall's trusted field inspectors so you can be sure that the information provided is always up to date. The Directory also includes a free and fully searchable CD-ROM (PC and Mac compatible) that enables you to search through Woodall's extensive database on your computer without being connected to the Internet. Best of all – Woodall's North American Directory also contains the most comprehensive listing of pet-welcome campgrounds in North America. For these and other reasons, we are confident that Camping and RVing with Dogs will become an essential asset to you as well as your dog. Happy trails and we hope to see you and your dog on the road.

 This symbol, appearing throughout the book, is used to highlight **important information.**

The Ten Commandments

These two Yorkies are enjoying the view from their campsite's picnic table.

Every worthwhile endeavor comes with an underlying collection of fundamental rules and associated priorities. When you are camping and RVing with your dog, these are some of the things that matter the most:

1. Make sure that your dog can't get lost

As full-time RVers, we invariably come across campers that have somehow lost track of their dog. In most cases, the dog is eventually found. However, in some cases, the family ends up going home without their dog. There is no way to describe the sorrow, the anxiety, and the despair that these families feel as they drive away. When you're on the road or staying in a campground, make absolutely sure that your dog is always in your control. If there was only one rule about camping and RVing with dogs – this would be it.

2. Get your dog's vaccinations up to date

Many campgrounds are located in wooded settings. As a result, it's not uncommon to encounter an animal with rabies. Similarly, if you decide to visit Canada or Mexico with your dog, you'll have to verify that they've had all their shots. If your dog gets into a serious fight with another dog, the crucial issue will be your dog's rabies shots. Likewise, if your dog (regrettably) bites someone, the first question will be about your dog's vaccinations. For these reasons, some campgrounds will ask to see a copy of your dog's vaccination records. So when you are packing for your next trip – be sure to bring a few extra copies.

3. Call the campground before you go

Even if a campground listing indicates that they're "pets-welcome" – always call ahead to confirm their actual policy regarding your dog(s). We have arrived at campgrounds with our two German Shepherd dogs only to find that "pets-welcome" meant dogs that weighed less than 20 pounds. In addition, some campgrounds charge a sizable fee for pets. If you call and inquire before you arrive, you'll be able to decide if it's a campground for the whole family.

4. Make pet safety your number one priority

For any number of reasons, dogs frequently get hurt and even lost when camping and RVing. In most cases, the situation could have been prevented with some common sense and a little planning. If you keep your dog on a leash at all times, you'll be off to a great start. In addition, the next chapter describes other effective ways to ensure that your dog returns home safe and sound.

5. Take responsibility for your dog

As it turns out, the biggest complaint about dogs at campgrounds has nothing to do with their bark, their bite, or their behavior. Instead, it's often the owners that are at fault. If you always pick up after your dog and keep them on a leash at all times, you won't give people much to complain about. You'll also make it a lot easier for other RVers that travel with dogs.

6. Learn about your immediate environment

North America is a vast continent with an amazing assortment of wildlife, plants, topography, and challenging environmental conditions. If you don't know what you're getting into – you might inadvertently be placing yourself and your dog in serious danger. Every year, countless numbers of dogs die from heatstroke, snake bites, bear attacks, drowning, and other unforeseen hazards. Smart campers and RVers take the time to learn about the environment they are camping in. This advice is particularly important if you expect to stay in a specific area for a while and plan to go on extended hikes with your dog.

7. Anticipate problems

We all know that in the real world – stuff happens. Yet few campers and RVers think about what they would actually do in a genuine emergency. For example, if you were involved in a serious traffic accident, what would you do with your dog? If your dog started to show signs of overheating while you were out hiking, how would you handle it? Likewise, if something were to happen to you while your dog was back at the campground, who would take care of him? How would they even know your dog was there? Fortunately, this book includes a number of effective ways to deal with these and other challenging scenarios. So before you leave on your next trip – make some plans to deal with the unexpected.

8. Involve your dog in everything you do

There is more to camping and RVing with dogs than simply bringing them along. If you really want your dog to have a good time, include them in all of your activities. Take them on long hikes. Let them play in the water. Throw a ball. Set up an obstacle course. Grill them up a hamburger (dogs prefer them well done). If you get the chance, participate in campground social activities like dog shows, dog play areas, and group hikes. If you make sure that your dog has a lot of fun – they'll probably help you pack the next time you decide to go on a trip.

9. Make it easy to find your dog

Even the best pet owners occasionally get separated from their dog. If your dog does get lost, the ability to make a positive ID will become crucial. For permanent identification purposes, have a vet implant a microchip under your dog's skin. For even more security, get your dog a collar that takes advantage of GPS technology. A dog wearing one of these high-tech devices can be tracked virtually anywhere with the help of a PC or a hand-held tracker. In any case, make sure that your dog wears a secure collar that has a tag with his name, your phone number, and the date of his last rabies vaccination. This book offers several other proven methods for finding a lost dog. More importantly – it includes a number of helpful suggestions designed to ensure that your dog doesn't get lost in the first place. We can't say enough about this issue.

10. Savor the experience

Dogs love the outdoors more than anything else. RVing and camping with your dog is a precious experience that will ultimately become one of your fondest memories. So the next time you are sitting around a campfire under the stars with your buddy, remember – this is RVing at its very best.

3

The Top Ten Rules of Dog Safety

Muffin owns the front seat in her family's motorhome (courtesy John and Phyllis Sadler).

When planning your next camping trip, safety should always be one of your top priorities. The following suggestions reflect the kinds of problems that can actually occur when camping and RVing with a dog. For further information, refer to the appropriate sections inside this book.

1. Don't let your dog go out without a leash

Nothing is more important than making sure your dog is always on a leash. Each year, thousands of dogs get loose, run away, and are never seen again. Some wander aimlessly until they die of exposure or exhaustion. Others are ultimately hit by vehicles, shot by hunters, or killed by

11

predators. In virtually every case, the dog's owner believed that a leash wasn't necessary (at the time). However, if you keep your dog on a leash at all times, you'll always know where they are. It's that simple.

2. Protect them from rabies and heartworm

When you're camping with your dog, they may come across animals that are capable of transmitting rabies. Animals considered to be at the highest risk of transmitting rabies to dogs include bats, skunks, foxes, raccoons, and coyotes (as well as other dogs). When a dog is bitten by a rabid animal, he can probably be saved if he's immediately taken to a veterinarian (for a series of injections). After the symptoms appear, however, no cure is possible. Heartworm, a parasitical disease of the heart muscle, is also incurable if the infestation has already taken hold. Fortunately, diseases like rabies and heartworm are entirely preventable. All you have to do is get your dog vaccinated and make sure he gets his heartworm medication.

3. Watch your dog when setting up camp

Setting up camp is usually an exciting time for everyone. However, statistics confirm that this is one of the most dangerous times for a dog. So before you back into a site, open a slide-out, drop your steps, put down your jacks, or unload an ATV – make sure that your dog is safely out of the way. Likewise, since your dog will be unfamiliar with his new surroundings, he will be more apt to get distracted, disoriented, and lost.

4. Check your batteries

Each year, numerous campers and their pets are killed by fire or carbon monoxide poisoning. Sadly, most of these tragedies could have been prevented with the help of commercially available detectors. All late-model RVs come with detectors that can monitor trace amounts of smoke, propane, and carbon monoxide. If your RV doesn't, install them right away. Then, be sure to test them several times a year. We install new batteries every year (whether they need it or not). It's a small price to pay for a little piece of mind. Also, if you're using a portable propane heater inside your tent, make sure there's enough fresh air to prevent the build-up of carbon monoxide. Since carbon monoxide is odorless, you won't know you have a problem until it's too late.

5. Keep an eye on your dog's behavior

You know your dog better than anyone else. As a result, you're more apt to notice subtle changes. If something doesn't look right, it probably isn't. Consequently, if you observe any of the following symptoms, get your dog to a veterinarian right away:

Inability to Urinate	Inexplicable Viciousness
Abnormal Lumps	Excessive Head Shaking
Abnormal Posture	Unable to Put Weight on a Limb
Excessive Drooling	Discharges from Nose or Eyes
Seizures	Unable to Stand or Get Up
Sudden Lethargy	Open Sores or Major Hair Loss
Marked Weight Loss	Inexplicable Anxiousness
Breathing Problems	Excessive Urination
Excessive Vomiting	Conspicuous Loss of Appetite
Severe Diarrhea	Persistent Constipation

6. Learn how to provide first aid to your dog

When a medical emergency occurs at home, you simply drive to your local vet. But if this same situation were to occur along a dark road in a strange town, it would be a whole different story. Although there are ways to get help while on the road, it always takes longer than you think. In the meantime, your ability to provide competent first aid could save your dog's life. The Pet E.R. Guide from Trailer Life Books (www.trailerlifedirectory.com) includes a state-by-state listing of pet care facilities, emergency animal hospitals, as well as other useful information.

7. Have an emergency action plan

History has proven over and over again that luck favors the prepared. In the Navy, sailors spend nearly all of their time preparing for various disaster scenarios. Then, if something were to actually happen, they know exactly what to do. When you're getting ready for your next trip, take the time to develop an emergency action plan for your family and your dog. This book describes how to prepare for and contend with a wide range of challenging situations. Read these sections carefully and develop a strategy of your own. Then, if you smell smoke, get a flat tire, or can't find your dog – you won't have to waste precious time figuring out what to do.

8. Watch the heat

With their thick coat, extended muzzles, and relatively high body temperature, dogs are able to remain relatively comfortable in very cold weather. However, these same traits also make them highly susceptible to a wide range of heat-related problems including dehydration and exposure. Consequently, avoid extended hikes and vigorous activities with your dog during warm weather. Likewise, never ever leave your dog in a vehicle during warm weather. If you have no choice (such as in an emergency), leave them lots of water and implement one or more of the emergency RV power back-up systems described further on in this book.

9. Avoid high-risk situations

One of the greatest things about camping and RVing is the fact that you can explore exciting new places and discover unusual environments. However, this also means that you could potentially place your dog in grave danger without actually knowing it. For example, if you hike into an area that contains poisonous snakes, your dog may not survive, especially if your dog is large. When a dog is bitten by a poisonous snake, he must normally get to a vet in less than an hour. However, if your dog tries to walk back to your vehicle, they will hasten their own death because of the resulting increase in their heart rate. At the same time, few people can carry a large dog over a long distance. Consequently, your dog will most likely die before getting help. If you plan on taking your dog into unfamiliar territory – first learn about the potential hazards and risks that you might face.

10. If your dog gets lost, don't panic

Even the most responsible pet owners sometimes lose track of their dog. If you suddenly notice that your dog is nowhere to be found, take the time to examine the situation. If you're near a wooded area, it's likely that your dog headed in that direction. Therefore, concentrate your efforts in that area. Similarly, if you're staying in a crowded park or campground, take advantage of the situation by putting up lost dog posters. Last but not least – think carefully before you jump in your car to go look for your dog. In many cases, the dogs are simply exploring their new environment. By driving away, you might unintentionally make things worse (if your dog comes back and nobody is there). If possible – stay in the immediate area where you last saw your dog and send someone else to perform a vehicle-based search.

Getting Ready for the Trip

These two children wouldn't dream of going
camping and RVing without their buddies.

This chapter describes the preparations you'll need to
make when getting ready for your camping and RVing
trip. Whether you're bringing one dog or a small pack, the
provisions described in this chapter are primarily designed
to keep your dog safe, secure, and comfortable while you are
on the road. As a result, this is one of the book's most
important chapters.

Things to Do Before You Go

The first time we decided to go RVing with our two dogs,
we had no idea what we were doing. To begin, our dogs had
never been in a motorhome before so when we got ready

to leave, one of our dogs refused to go up the steps. When he finally decided to join us on our maiden journey, he was so frightened – he crawled under the front seat and stayed there for the entire trip. The only time he came out was to devour one of the seatbelts while we were out getting some groceries. That was five years ago and needless to say – we've all come a long way since then.

As it turns out, there's a lot more to camping and RVing with dogs than simply taking them along for the ride. In fact, I would argue that when it comes to traveling and camping with dogs – skillful preparations and focused knowledge could literally save your dog's life. I know this because I've personally witnessed the often unforgiving consequences of ignorance, negligence, and poor planning. That being said, once you fully understand what it takes to ensure that your dog is safe, healthy, and happy – you'll never want to go camping and RVing without them.

Bring your Dog to the Vet

Taking your dog to the vet before you leave will minimize problems during the trip.

Before you leave, schedule a visit to your local veterinarian for a thorough check-up. Even if you're only going for a short trip, it will give you an opportunity to confirm that your dog is healthy. While there, take care of any unresolved medical issues, and bring all of your dog's vaccinations up to date. If you're planning to stay in an area that has mosquitoes – make sure your dog is tested for heartworm disease. Assuming they are free of the disease, purchase an ample supply of heartworm medication and any other medicine your dog requires. In addition, ask for a written prescription just in case you run out. In addition, check to see if your dog is up to date on their flea and tick medication. It's no fun finding fleas and ticks on your dog, let alone in your RV.

If your dog's diet includes any specialized products, stock up before you hit the road. It may be harder than you think to find the items away from home. One of our dogs requires a special dog food (Hill's Prescription Diet®). As full-time RVers, we've spent countless hours chasing down animal hospitals that carry this specialized product.

While at the vet, you might also want to consider getting an ID microchip surgically embedded under your dog's skin. The microchip will make it easier to identify your dog if they get lost and then picked up. For details, please refer to the section further on in this chapter titled "The Best Ways to Find a Lost Dog". Finally, take a few business cards from your vet, just in case you need to give them a call.

KENNEL COUGH
If you're planning to enter your dog in a dog show, make sure they're treated for kennel cough. Kennel cough is a highly contagious respiratory illness that is prevalent when groups of dogs are kept in close quarters.

Get a Copy of your Dog's Vaccination Records

Obtain a few copies of your dog's vaccination records. Make

sure that it clearly shows when they have had their last rabies shots. The vet should also give you a rabies tag that indicates the date of your dog's most recent vaccination. Attach this tag securely to your dog's collar. Then, put a copy of your dog's vaccination records in a convenient location such as your vehicle's glove box. You may end up staying at a campground that requires written proof of your dog's rabies vaccination. Chapter 9 includes a pet health record form that will help you to document your dog's vaccination history.

CROSSING THE BORDER INTO MEXICO OR CANADA
One of the best things about camping and RVing is the fact that you can change your travel plans anytime you wish. However, if you decide to cross into Canada or Mexico with a dog, you'll need a rabies vaccination certificate that is signed by a licensed veterinarian. The certificate must show that your dog was vaccinated at least 30 days before crossing the border. In addition, the certificate must also include an expiration date. In rare cases, your dog may even be examined at the port of entry to make sure they are free of any communicable diseases.

Give them a Bath

If at all possible, give your dog a bath and a good brushing before you leave. The bath will help to keep their skin and coat in good shape and the brushing will reduce the volume of fur in your vehicle. Better yet, take them to the groomers for an overhaul. Your dog will feel better and look their best. A few years ago, we took our dogs to the groomers for a shampoo and a thorough brushing. When we picked them up, they looked (and smelled) like they had just won the

Westminster Kennel Club dog show. Two days later, they were both up to their waist in smelly black mud along the banks of a small pond. Dogs will be dogs.

Making Sure your Dog Never Gets Lost

Any time you take a dog out of their regular environment – there is always a chance that they might get lost. Therefore, when you're making plans to go camping or RVing with your dog, you'll need to find a way to make sure this doesn't happen. As a practical matter, pet security strategies fall into one of two basic groups. One is designed to prevent a dog from getting lost in the first place. The other is intended to find a dog that has already gone astray. Each strategy is discussed below:

 ## Always Use a Leash

There are two proven methods for ensuring that your dog never gets lost. The first is the unremitting use of a leash. After all, a dog can't get lost if they're always kept on a leash.

As full-time RVers with two dogs, we've had our share of oversights and close calls. As a result, we now have one overriding rule about camping and RVing with our dogs: they never go outside without a leash. In fact, whenever we take our dogs for a walk – we always attach the leash to their collar before we open the door.

CHEWING THEIR WAY TO FREEDOM
Not all leashes are the same. We used to use leashes that consisted of a three quarter-inch strip of rugged woven fabric. However, one of our dogs discovered that he could easily bite the leash in half with his back teeth. The last time it happened, I was standing in a park and noticed a nice looking dog with a short section of leash dangling from his collar. After burning through two more leashes, we finally switched to chain.

Occasionally, we've stepped outside only to find another dog exploring our campsite. If our dogs weren't already on a leash, things could get tense. Of course, we now glance outside to see if the coast is clear but they're still always kept on a leash. The only exception is when they're in a fenced enclosure.

SKUNK SEASON

Every autumn, the skunks come out at dusk to grub for cutworms and beetles. If your dog isn't on a leash, he may decide to investigate the cute little creature with the white stripe. When your dog gets squirted in the face by that cute little creature, he'll have difficulty breathing and seeing. But that's just the beginning.

No matter what you use to wash your dog, it will be several weeks before the stench goes away completely. In the meantime, your dog will spend every day and every night alone outside because of the odor. Always use a leash – especially during skunk season.

Train your Dog

The other method for ensuring that your dog never gets lost is to train them to come when they are called. If a dog has been taught to respond to the "come" command – they will rarely run away from their owners. However, there are circumstances when even a trained dog will run off and get lost. One of the most common scenarios occurs when a dog chases another animal such as a deer. In their instinctive mind-set, a dog may chase the animal for several miles only to find themselves completely disoriented.

While training is clearly one of the best ways to keep a dog under control, it's still not a substitute for a leash. We always keep an extra leash in our car and one in our RV – just in case we can't find their regular leashes. Chapter 7 describes the various types of pet containment solutions that are currently available to dog owners (while staying at a campground). Please refer to this chapter while you're planning your trip. That way, you'll know exactly what to bring.

GET OUT YOUR CAMERA
Before leaving, take a few snapshots of your dog. You may be able to use your cell phone if it has a built-in camera.

Then, store the image in a safe place. If your dog ever gets lost, you'll be able to use the photo to create "lost pet" posters. The photo will also be useful for showing other people what your dog looks like.

The Best Ways to Keep Track of your Dog

While camping and RVing over the years, we have sadly witnessed more than our share of people that have lost their dogs. In some cases, they're lucky enough to find them. In other situations, they aren't so fortunate. The worst place to lose a dog is in the desert. Between the heat, the cactus, and the coyotes – you don't have much time to find your dog. On that note, while you're getting ready, consider taking advantage of some of the solutions that are used today to help locate a lost dog. We'll start with the simplest options and go up from there:

| **Traditional ID Tags** | Personalized ID tags can be ordered from veterinarians and pet stores. In addition, many pet supply retailers now have vending machines that are capable of producing engraved pet ID tags while you wait. The tag should include the dog's name as well as a current phone number. Some owners are also adding an e-mail address. If you become a member of The Good Sam Club (**www.goodsamclub.com**), you can participate in their pet finder program at no extra cost. Participants receive an engraved dog tag that includes a toll-free number. If someone finds your |

dog, they can simply call the number and The Good Sam Club will contact you with the good news. Regardless of what other methods you use, make sure that your dog's collar includes an ID tag with accurate and current contact information. Then, make sure that your dog's collar fits snuggly (there should be room for two fingers). Needless to say – an ID tag won't be much help if your dog loses his collar.

Electronic Dog Tags	You can now store detailed information about your dog on an electronic dog tag that attaches to your dog's collar. Inserted into the USB port of any computer or laptop – these durable, waterproof devices utilize ready-to-use forms to enter detailed data about your dog's medical requirements, contact information, and anything else you can think of. One example is the Top Tag Electronic Pet ID Tag (**www.americas-pet-store.com**).
Embedded Microchips	ID Microchips have been used to identify lost pets for several years. The microchip (about the size of a grain of rice) includes a unique identification code. It's typically implanted between the shoulder blades of the dog. The identification code along with information about the dog is then added to a national database that's available 24 hours a day, 365 days a year. When a lost pet is found, it can be scanned at an animal shelter or by a

participating veterinarian. The dog's ID code is then entered into the database and the pet owner is immediately notified. To date, hundreds of thousands of dogs have been reunited with their owners as a result of this technology. Most vets charge less than $100 to embed a microchip. Unlike a pet ID tag, embedded microchips still work if the dog loses its collar.

GPS Enabled Dog Collars

Modern GPS technology has finally come to the rescue for finding lost pets. The typical system comes with a waterproof collar that includes a built-in transmitter as well as an antenna. A hand-held receiver is then used to track the lost dog.

Top-rated models can successfully track a dog up to seven miles away, depending on the terrain. While these devices won't work if your dog loses their collar – they are well-designed and utilize sturdy buckles that are difficult to unfasten. Check out **www.gpsdogcollartracking.com**. Since they have a good selection, it's a good place to start.

Packing

Storage space is almost always at a premium when camping and RVing so it will be important to prioritize when you are packing for your trip. One useful approach is to purchase see-through plastic storage bins that are appropriately sized for the items you're bringing. For example, we keep their medications, a flea comb, a pet brush, nail clippers, and pet shampoo in a small plastic bin that fits under our motorhome's bathroom vanity. Similarly, we store most of our dog's dry food in a large bin in one of the RV's cargo bays. In addition, we keep a week's supply of food in a smaller bin that sits next to our dogs' food bowls. When the small bin is empty, we simply refill it from the larger bin.

In any case, there is one universal rule about storing things in an RV: continue to rearrange your stuff until your system is perfectly situated and convenient to use. If you find that you're wasting a lot of time searching for things – make the necessary improvements until everything functions smoothly. Eventually, you'll have an arrangement that's perfect for both you as well as your dog.

A Ready-to-use Check-List for your Dog

Check-lists are the most effective way to ensure that you bring the things you need. You can start with this one:

❏ Collar with ID and Rabies Tags

❏ Containers for Food

❏ Description of Dog's Tattoo

- ❑ Dog Bed
- ❑ Dog Blanket
- ❑ Dog Booties
- ❑ Dog Leashes
- ❑ Dog Treats
- ❑ Dog Food and Extra Water
- ❑ Flea and Tick Comb
- ❑ Flea and Tick Medication
- ❑ Food and Spill-proof Water Bowl
- ❑ Heartworm Medication
- ❑ Pertinent Medical Records
- ❑ Proof of Rabies Vaccination
- ❑ Screw-in Tie-out Anchor
- ❑ GPS Tracking Device
- ❑ Orange Scarf (for hunting season)
- ❑ Nail Clippers
- ❑ Clothing (for dogs)
- ❑ Dog Brush
- ❑ Pet Crate
- ❑ Pet First-Aid Kit
- ❑ Dog Shampoo
- ❑ Dog Toys (and toy box)
- ❑ Photo of Your Dog(s)
- ❑ Pet Waste Bags
- ❑ Special Medications
- ❑ Insect Repellent
- ❑ Primary Vet's Telephone Number
- ❑ Flashlight (rechargeable)
- ❑ Pet Fencing (or equivalent)

Handling Unique Travel Considerations

In an ideal setting, everyone would have healthy, well-adjusted dogs that were ready to go anywhere and handle anything without any complications. However, in the real world – life isn't that simple. Therefore, this section covers the more challenging side of camping and RVing with dogs.

Fearful Dogs

For any number of reasons, some dogs have a difficult time adjusting to an RV. Typically, the dog will be afraid to enter the vehicle or when they do – they often hide under a table or behind a chair. Luckily, there are some effective ways to help your dog overcome their fears. For starters, park your RV in your driveway; leave the door open; and go in and out as many times as possible. In addition, put some food and water in the RV (near the door) so they know it's all right to go in. Do everything you can to minimize the level of importance associated with the vehicle. Don't raise your voice and never force them into the RV. The idea is to reduce their anxiety, not amplify it. When they do finally enter the RV – reward them with praise and give them a treat.

 If your dog still hesitates to enter your camper or RV, try to find out what they might be afraid of. It could be the engine so try turning it off. If they're afraid of the vehicle's steps, consider using a ramp or cover the steps with a towel. Some people put their dogs in a crate and carry them into the vehicle. Others have put a cat

or another dog in the RV to make the vehicle more tempting. Since the main idea is to have fun – take your time. With a little patience, your dog will eventually forget all about their fears.

To help your dog get accustomed to staying in your RV, sit with them while it is parked somewhere. Then, take them for a few short trips to get them comfortable with the environment. If they're still anxious, spend a night or two in the RV with your dog. This way, they'll see that the vehicle is simply an extension of their regular home. In any case, relax. Like you, your dog will eventually learn to love their new house on wheels.

Disabled and Older Dogs

While most RVs are surprisingly comfortable and well designed, there are a few problems for dogs that have difficulty in getting around. For starters, RV entrance steps are notoriously inadequate and excessively steep – especially if the vehicle is up on jacks. We had a large dog with severe hip problems that could barely make it up the steps in our motorhome. To fix the problem, we instituted two solutions, depending on the circumstances. If the RV had to be raised up during the leveling process, we installed a set of steps that were made out of wood. The motorhome's regular steps were retracted to accommodate the wooden ones. Today, you can now purchase portable RV steps that can be quickly disassembled for easy transport and storage when you're ready to hit the road.

If the RV wasn't jacked up too high, we used a simple ramp constructed from a piece of plywood. Fortunately, portable lightweight ramps can also be purchased at many pet stores. Most of these ramps can be folded to facilitate handling and storage. To minimize slipping (especially in wet weather), we attached anti-slip strips. Available at most home supply chains, these strips resemble rugged pieces of coarse sandpaper that can be attached to any surface with a crack-and-peel adhesive backing. Although it took a little while for our dog to get used to the substitute steps and the ramp – they ultimately enabled him to get in and out of the RV without any problems.

Another common problem for disabled dogs is slippery floors. As it turns out, many dogs have difficulty walking on linoleum or tile flooring because of slipping. For disabled or older dogs, this type of flooring represents a genuine hazard. The solution, of course, is to cover the floor with carpeting. However, it is virtually impossible to adequately cover linoleum or tile with carpeting unless you use an adhesive or carpet tacks. Instead, most RVers put down small throw rugs that are even more dangerous than the underlying floor. If you have a dog that is apt to get injured from slippery floors – have your floor replaced with carpeting. It may seem excessive at the time but it'll be a lot cheaper than paying for an orthopedic surgeon to re-build your dog's knee.

Dogs with Motion Sickness

Years ago, we had a standard poodle, named Jake, who would begin to drool excessively whenever he entered a vehicle. We tried everything from window shades and medication to soothing music and treats. However, the more we tried, the more he drooled. Fortunately for Jake, we had a vet that performed house calls as part of a mobile veterinarian service. In the sixteen years that we lived with Jake, he went in the car less than half a dozen times. When we took Jake to the vet for his final voyage – he drooled the entire way.

Technically, motion sickness is caused by vibration that occurs within a dog's inner ear when the vehicle is in motion. When this happens, your dog feels dizzy and soon becomes nauseous. Some dogs tend to drool, others vomit, and a few even develop diarrhea. Luckily, there are a number of ways to alleviate motion sickness in a dog. For starters, begin taking your dog on frequent short trips in your vehicle, camper, or RV. Then, gradually increase the length of the ride. In many cases, this technique has successfully eliminated motion sickness altogether.

If this approach doesn't work with your dog, you may want to give anti-nausea medication a try. Frequently used medications include diphenhydramine (Benadryl®), meclizine (Bonine®), and dimenhydrinate (Dramamine®). All three of these over-the-counter medications are available without a prescription. However, before you give any medication to your dog, always discuss the issue with your veterinarian; that way, they'll be able to determine the proper dosage (for your dog) and identify any potential side-effects that might occur.

Some owners have been able to treat motion sickness with sedatives (for the dog, not you). Commonly used sedatives include acepromazine and phenobarbital. These medications are available by prescription and should be used with caution because of the potential risk associated with side effects.

MOTION SICKNESS
If your dog suffers from motion sickness, don't feed them or give them much water before you leave. You might also try limiting their view of the outside (while traveling) by either keeping them in a crate or by closing the blinds in your RV. Sooner or later — most dogs learn to ride in a vehicle without getting sick.

Shedding

Camping and RVing with a dog can be a real challenge if your dog has a tendency to shed a lot. For a while, we were filling a vacuum cleaner bag every week with fur. However, if you brush your dog every day, you'll drastically reduce the amount of fur you have to cope with. This is especially important during shedding season – which occurs in early spring in most regions of the country.

The other "trick" for managing pet fur is to cover the seats in your vehicle with tightly woven fabric or plastic. This will enable you to keep most of the dog fur on the floor where it can be vacuumed.

Aggressive Dogs and Controversial Breeds

If your dog likes to bark at other dogs, you are not alone. On the other hand, if your dog behaves aggressively towards people – keep them at home. People go camping and RVing to have fun and relax. The last thing they want is to be

Pit Bulls can make great pets but some campgrounds ban this breed altogether.

terrified every time they walk by your campsite. Also, some campgrounds ban specific breeds so if you own a Rottweiler, a Pit Bull, or a Doberman pinscher, be sure to call before you leave to verify their policy. In addition, make sure you read Chapters 6 and 7. They describe some of the issues involved in choosing a campground as well as provide a number of useful suggestions for containing and controlling your dog while at a campground.

Preparing for Full-time RVing with Dogs

As full-time RVers with two dogs and a small collection of cats, we've had our share of slip-ups and lessons about camping and RVing with animals. Yet, we can't imagine what it would be like to travel or live in an RV without a dog. In addition to offering companionship and a repository for leftovers, dogs provide unsurpassed protection from a wide range of potential problems. While serious crime is virtually insignificant in campgrounds and RV parks – dogs can give you the peace of mind you might need when spending the night in a Wal-Mart parking lot.

These two dogs provide protection as well as companionship.

WORKING DOGS
If you're planning to get a dog for protection, research the various breeds to see which one would best suit your overall needs. While all dogs provide some level of protection and deterrence – there are certain breeds that are highly suited to do the task.

With respect to preparations, the process is generally the same whether you're planning a two week vacation or preparing to live in your RV for the next five years. However, there are a few key distinctions associated with full-time RVing that should be mentioned.

When getting ready for full-time RVing with dogs, pay close attention to the issue of space. It's fairly easy to steer clear of a dog bed for a week or two. On the other hand, it's impossible to avoid an obstacle for several years. When planning for full-time RVing with a dog – take the time to do things right.

If your RV has to go into the shop for lengthy repairs, you'll probably have to make arrangements for your dog. Many service shops will allow you to stay in your RV at night while they perform the repairs during the day. However, you'll still need to take your dog with you during the day. Alternatively, you might want to consider staying in a motel. Luckily, many inexpensive chains (i.e. Motel 6) permit pets.

In a small living area, everyone (including your dog) is competing for floor space. Therefore, from the start, let your dog know exactly where his space is. For example, our dogs have two specific areas where they can sleep without being disturbed. That way, we aren't constantly disrupting their routines.

When you're packing your RV, try not to bring a years' supply of pet food or enough medication to last a lifetime. You'll have plenty of chances to purchase additional supplies plus you'll need the storage space for other things.

When full-time RVing with dogs, you'll need more than your trusty little dust buster. We carry a canister vacuum cleaner, a carpet shampooer, and a good supply of replacement bags. When you're camping during mud season or your dog throws up on your carpet, you'll be glad you have an arsenal of heavy-duty cleaning tools.

Preparing Your Vehicle for the Trip

The last step in getting ready is to make sure that your vehicle is in good condition and adequately outfitted for camping and RVing with a dog. The next chapter (Chapter 5) describes the various options that are available when traveling with a dog. In the meantime, these are some of the more important tasks:

Obtain an emergency roadside service plan

When you're traveling with your dog and something goes wrong like a flat tire, you're going to need help getting back on the road again. That's why an emergency roadside assistance plan should be an integral part of every camping and RVing trip. One of the best is the Good Sam RV Emergency Road Service. Designed specifically for RVers – the service includes 24/7 toll-free emergency dispatch and towing service (using special equipment designed for RVs), flat tire service, lock-out protection, jump-starts, and fuel delivery. In addition, the Good Sam RV Emergency Road Service also provides $1200 trip interruption assistance as well as emergency medical referral support. At less than $100 for an entire year – their emergency road service is a real bargain.

ROADSIDE SERVICE PLANS WITH LOTS OF DOGS
If you're transporting large numbers of dogs, you may encounter a problem when obtaining a roadside service plan. Specifically, many roadside assistance companies will not service an RV that contains several dogs. The issue isn't entirely clear but many RVers have been refused service when they mention the fact that they're traveling with several dogs. Consequently, talk to the organization that is providing the plan to see if there are any pet-related restrictions. Some will require you to obtain a "commercial" roadside assistance plan. As expected, the price is normally higher than a regular plan.

Maintain your vehicle	When you're traveling with a dog – you don't really want any surprises. A well maintained vehicle is safer and more reliable than one that isn't. Therefore, take the time to review your vehicle's maintenance schedule and make sure everything has been taken care of. Have your tires examined and check to see that they're properly inflated for your vehicle. Similarly, have a service center check your batteries to make sure they're functioning properly and in good condition. You don't want to have electrical problems while on the road.
Carry a spare	If you have room for a spare tire, carry one. Even though some garages can provide a replacement, many don't carry the larger sizes that are typically used with RVs. This is particularly true in isolated regions of the country. If you don't have room for a spare, consider carrying just the tire. It will be a lot cheaper than purchasing a new tire.

Preparing your Vehicle for a Dog

Regardless of the vehicle or RV you have, there will always be a few preparations that should be made. If you're towing a trailer, fifth wheel, or pop-up, your dog will most likely travel with you in your tow vehicle. If you're traveling in a motorhome or a camping van, your dog will presumably be staying in the RV with you. In either case, the following products are designed to make life a little easier for both of you:

Seat Covers ~ Search for "pet seat covers" on the Internet and you'll discover a world of useful products for those of us that travel with dogs. We have a cover that fits snuggly over the rear seat of our minivan. The vinyl cover resists dog fur and prevents our dog's nails from damaging the underlying seats. Initially, the idea of purchasing seat covers seemed extravagant. Now, we wouldn't have a vehicle without them.

Pet Barriers ~ Pet barriers are designed to keep your dog from entering the front section of your vehicle. Some are made of metal while others consist of netting that is stretched across the width of your vehicle's interior. In any case, they're great to have when approaching toll booths, drive up windows, and other opportunities for the RVing dog.

Auxiliary Steps ~ As dogs get older, they often have some difficulty when getting in and out of a vehicle. Likewise, if you have a dog that is disabled, you should seriously consider getting some supplementary steps. Available from most pet stores, these portable steps are lightweight and can easily be kept in a trunk or in the back of a pickup truck. Alternatively, you can also find portable ramps that are specifically designed for dogs. Typically made of aluminum – these lightweight ramps often fold up for convenient storage and trouble-free handling.

Spill-proof Water Bowls ~ Handling food and

Spill-proof bowls keep the water where it belongs – no matter how rough the ride.

water in a car or a truck is problematic because of spillage. As a consequence, many campers and RVers wait until they're at a rest stop before giving their dog any food or water. However, there is another option – spill-proof pet bowls. These cleverly designed bowls are designed to hold water without spilling their contents. Available at many pet stores – these bowls utilize a curved top that traps water like an automobile tire. For their food, look for a heavy ceramic bowl with a flat bottom. The heavy weight will keep the bowl in place and the flat bottom will prevent it from tipping over and spilling the food. You may also want to place the bowl on non-slip shelf lining to prevent it from sliding around.

Dog Booster Seats ~ Dog booster seats are designed to give your dog a better view and a more comfortable ride in any vehicle. Normally suitable for dogs up to 40 lbs. – they are often padded and have a removable interior liner for washing. Some also include a zippered, front storage pocket, and a safety leash. You can find them at a few retail pet stores in addition to the Internet (**www.americas-pet-store.com**).

Dog Cargo Covers ~ If your dog spends much time in an SUV or a minivan, you should seriously consider getting a cargo area travel liner. Designed for comfort and safety, these liners normally conform to the shape of your vehicle's rear cargo area. The better ones utilize thick, soft quilted materials that feature a water-repellent top layer and a durable nylon bottom lining. To keep the cargo liner in place, most use slip-free pads. Available at various pet and auto accessory stores – you can also find these liners at **www.autoanything.com**.

Carpet and Furniture Covers – Dogs can be hard on upholstered furniture and carpeting. If your RV has carpeting that's difficult to clean, consider putting down a plastic runner. Likewise, an inexpensive slipcover will protect your sofa from unwanted dirt and fur. At a minimum, put a coarse floor mat just inside your RV's entrance door. It will catch a lot of dirt and mud that would otherwise end up on your carpet.

CLEANING TOOLS FOR REAL CAMPERS WITH DOGS
If you're planning to bring a dog (or two) on your next extended camping trip, consider bringing a full-size vacuum cleaner. Your enduring little dust buster is fine for a weekend at the shore but on a real camping trip, it'll choke on all that mud and fur.

Feeding

If you're traveling in a motorhome or a camping van, food and water is generally a minor issue. However, you'll need to devise a system to ensure that your dog always has a dependable supply of food and fresh water while you are traveling. We keep a few days' worth of dry food in a covered container that sits near our dog's food bowls. We then refill the container from a larger supply that's kept in our RV's cargo bin. The food in the cargo bin is stored in a sealed plastic container to keep out insects, rodents, and moisture. Always bring a plentiful supply of your dog's favorite food when you go camping. If you switch brands while on the road, your dog may experience serious digestive problems. You'll want to devise your own system but make sure that it's practical and convenient. Since it's a daily task – feeding your dog should be quick and easy.

This special feeding stand will keep your dog's food bowls in place.

For feeding, we use a wood stand that keeps the bowls from sliding around when traveling. The stand also makes it easier for large breed dogs to reach their food. Evidently, it significantly reduces the level of stress on their front legs.

Drinking Water

Fresh, clean drinking water is one of the keys to keeping your dog healthy and fit. However, even if you normally stay at reputable RV parks and campgrounds, you may not always have a reliable source of drinking water. Water filters can often improve the taste and odor of a water supply – but most filters aren't technically designed to eliminate dangerous pathogens or harmful contaminants. You can purchase water disinfecting tablets, but they'll have little effect on chemical contamination. In our travels, we've encountered water that is so salty or so full of minerals – it's literally undrinkable. In some cases, our dogs and cats won't even touch it. No matter what, always let the water run for thirty seconds or so before attaching your hose to a campground water supply. This will flush out any sediment that has accumulated in the pipes.

In some campgrounds, it's virtually impossible to find good tasting water.

When we do stay in places with bad tasting drinking water, we keep a water cooler in our RV that dispenses cold water from refillable jugs. The water coolers are available from Lowe's and The Home Depot. We typically get the jugs filled at water dispensing machines that are located in grocery stores or The Home Depot. Alternatively, you can find inexpensive drinking water in one-gallon plastic containers at supermarkets or discount stores like Wal-Mart. At around 75 cents a gallon, it's a reasonable alternative to a dubious water supply. Lastly, you might also want to look into reverse osmosis

(RO) water treatment systems. They're capable of producing substantial quantities of safe drinking water from virtually any source. To learn more about these systems, check out The RV Water Filter Store (**www.rvwaterfilterstore.com**).

If you have an RV or an auxiliary water tank, fill your tank (or some containers) before heading out. Keep in mind – a medium-size dog requires more than a gallon of fresh water each day. When filling your tank, always use a good water filter and be sure to disinfect your water storage system periodically.

For our dogs, we use spill-proof bowls because they keep the water in, no matter how rough the ride. When we get to the campground – we switch to a larger stainless steel bowl that holds more water and is easier to clean. Their water bowl is always kept on a plastic placemat that protects the floor by containing spills.

HOW TO DISINFECT WATER FOR DRINKING
If you're required to use water that may not be safe for drinking, boil the water for 3 minutes. Alternatively, add 8 drops of household bleach to each gallon. Mix the treated water thoroughly and allow it to stand, preferably covered, for 30 minutes. The water should have a slight chlorine odor. If not, repeat the dosage and allow the water to stand for an additional 15 minutes. If the treated water has too strong a chlorine taste — allow the water to stand exposed to the air for a few hours or pour it from one clean container to another several times (to aerate the water).

Sleeping Accommodations

It doesn't take a government study to realize that dogs like to be as comfortable as possible when they sleep. Fortunately, dog beds are inexpensive and readily available. Some campers (who will remain nameless) let their dogs sleep with them on their bed. Others bring an extra air mattress for their tent. Whatever solution you decide to use, make sure it's comfortable. Also, cover their bed with something that can be easily laundered. However, before you add the cover to the laundry – give it a good shake outside to remove as much dog fur as possible. Otherwise, you may find dog fur in all of your nice clean clothes.

Dog Toys

When we brought home our first German Shepherd dog many years ago, we bought them a few toys at a pet store. To our delight, she played with these toys for hours on end. We came to realize that dogs, like children, require toys in order

DOG TOYS TO AVOID
Stay away from rawhide chews, real bones, and toys that contain a squeaking mechanism. According to The American Veterinary Medical Association (AVMA), these items top the list as the most dangerous items to chew on. Apparently, the rawhide chews have a tendency to produce intestinal blockages. Likewise, real bones can splinter and subsequently damage a dog's digestive tract. Lastly, the squeaking mechanisms in dog toys have a tendency to get lodged in their throat. It makes you wonder why these items are still sold.

to stay active and entertained. Some chew toys can even help to keep your dog's teeth clean. So before you hit the road – purchase some pet toys and a suitable box to hold them all. Your dog will derive endless enjoyment rummaging through the box looking for their favorite chew toy.

Preparing for Problems

At some point during your travels, you may encounter a problem while on the road. It could be a flat tire, an empty fuel tank, a minor accident, or something that requires your vehicle to be towed to a repair shop. In any case, when a problem does occur – having a dog can complicate matters, particularly if you're not prepared.

Therefore, this section is specifically designed to help you achieve two crucial objectives. The first entails reducing the risk of a problem occurring in the first place. The second involves developing a contingency plan to keep your dog safe and out of the way until you're back on the road.

Dog-proofing your RV

The first step in reducing the possibility of a problem is to safety-proof your RV's interior so your dog can't get hurt. While most campers and RVs are inherently safe in terms of obvious hazards, it always pays to take a close look around to eliminate any hidden risks that you might miss. For starters, look for heavy objects that can fall while you're traveling. One of our dogs had a close call with a laser printer that was poorly secured. Fortunately, the printer missed the dog but for several weeks – she refused to go anywhere near the offending piece of hardware. Similarly, we had a bookshelf that ejected all of its books when we came to a sudden stop. Keep in mind, when you're driving down the road – unpredictable things can happen at any time.

Making Sure your Dog Can't Escape

While you're at it – search for and eliminate any possible pathways to the outside. This will typically include heating and cooling ducts, and windows without screens. We once had a kitten that escaped through a hidden opening underneath the bathroom vanity in our motorhome. As it turned out – the opening was part of the RV's plumbing system. Although we searched for days, we unfortunately never found the kitten. A small dog could've easily made its way through the concealed opening as well.

We lost our cat Rosie when she escaped through a hidden opening in our motorhome.

If your RV has a screen door, consider installing a protective grill to prevent your dog from accidentally breaking through the screen. Our dogs ripped the screen in our motorhome's entrance door in no time. We replaced the screen and purchased a screen door grate from Camping World. You can also find "pet-proof" screening at most home supply or hardware stores. This heavy-duty plastic screening is considerably thicker than traditional vinyl screening. The one disadvantage is the fact that it's harder to see through than conventional window screening.

Eliminating Safety Hazards

In addition, look for things that could potentially snag your dog's collar. Each year, a significant number of dogs are accidentally strangled in this manner. If you have a puppy or a very immature dog, you'll also need to "puppy-proof" your camper or RV. Our full-grown German Shepherd male literally devoured one of our seatbelts – buckle and all. We made the mistake of keeping their toy box next to the front seat and we suspect he mistook the seatbelt for one of his toys.

In the same way, always keep household chemicals and cleaning agents out of reach and avoid using extension cords, if possible. Child-proof cabinet latches are highly effective for keeping a dog out of a cupboard. When looking for potential hazards – try to be imaginative without becoming paranoid.

This amusing sign lets others know that there are dogs inside.

In the event of an emergency, rescue workers will need to know exactly what they're dealing with. Therefore, put up a sign on the door (or window) of your RV that lists the number and type of animals that are inside. Conversely, visit a pet store and purchase a ready-to-use "Pets Inside" sign.

Detecting Fire, Carbon Monoxide, and Propane

In 2007, an entire family of RVers (along with their dog) in Michigan died from carbon monoxide poisoning as they slept in their beds. Evidently, they were using a portable space heater that somehow malfunctioned. To make matters worse, their RV had a working carbon monoxide detector but the battery was missing.

Today, carbon monoxide, smoke, and propane detectors are mandatory in all new recreational vehicles. If your vehicle lacks any of these devices – go out and purchase one today. In addition, always check them every month to make sure the batteries are still operative.

 ALWAYS USE SEPARATE DETECTORS
Even though some manufacturers sell combined carbon monoxide and propane detectors, always use separate detectors. The reason has to do with the fact that carbon monoxide detectors must be installed on the ceiling while propane detectors must always be located at the base of a wall.

Medical Emergencies

Chapter 9 is focused on the issue of dog medical care and includes ways to deal with medical emergencies. However, there are a number of things that you can do before you leave that could help in the case of a medical emergency.

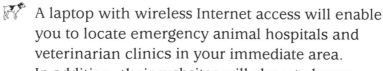 A laptop with wireless Internet access will enable you to locate emergency animal hospitals and veterinarian clinics in your immediate area. In addition, their websites will almost always include driving directions to reduce the probability of getting lost. Last but not least – the Internet can be very helpful for diagnosing and treating

CELL PHONES – THE BEST TOOL FOR ANY EMERGENCY
The best tool for dealing with any emergency on the road is a cell phone. If you plan on driving in areas that may have limited service, look into having a cell phone antenna installed. The leading manufacturer of cell phone amplification technology is Wilson Electronics (**www.wilsonelectronics.com**). Their RV/Trucker Roof Mount Cellular Antenna (Model 301119) is used by thousands of RVers and long-haul truckers. It's a great product and will ensure that you have cell phone service from virtually anywhere. We've used their antenna for years and as a result – we've never been out of range.

certain medical problems.

🐾 "The Pet E.R. Guide" from Trailer Life Books (**www.trailerlifedirectory.com**) includes a state-by-state listing of pet care facilities, emergency animal hospitals, as well as other useful information. Don't leave home without it.

🐾 Compile and bring a dog first aid kit. Chapter 9 lists the items that should be included in the kit.

🐾 Don't switch your dog's food when packing for your trip. This may trigger gastrointestinal problems such as gas, diarrhea, or vomiting.

🐾 Plan to keep your dog comfortable during the trip. If it's warm outside, use air conditioning or open a few windows. Also, give your dog plenty of water and be sure to stop periodically to give them a chance to take a short walk. If your dog is comfortable – they're less likely to become ill.

🐾 Chapter 9 includes a pet health record form that will enable you to document your dog's vaccination history as well as any other relevant medical information.

Accidents

No one wants to think about the possibility of getting into an accident. However, as the saying goes, expect the best and prepare for the worst. Here are some tips from emergency response professionals:

🐾 The key to surviving an accident is to stay in your seat. Always wear a seatbelt and keep your doors locked. This will drastically increase your odds of staying alive and remaining in control.

🐾 When you're calling 911 for help, tell the dispatcher that you have a dog. This way, they can contact animal control to make sure your dog is kept safe.

🐾 If you are in a collision but still able to function, secure your dog as quickly as possible. Due to fear, most dogs will attempt to flee the scene after an accident. In many cases, they are impossible to locate.

🐾 If you plan on driving in a high risk setting (i.e. the Los Angeles expressway), consider putting your dog in a crate. It's the safest place for a dog during an accident.

BUCKLE UP (YOUR DOG)
You can now purchase a seat belt for your dog. They're typically made from a synthetic material that is strength-rated, but provides a slight amount of stretch to absorb shock in the case of a sudden stop. Most are designed to function with your vehicle's seat belt tensioning device, thus providing some range of motion while traveling. However, in the case of a sudden stop (or a collision) it locks in place to keep your dog secure. You can find these seat belts at some retail pet stores as well as on the web (www.americas-pet-store.com).

Highway Breakdowns

This portable pet crate is perfect for keeping small dogs safe and out of the way.

If your vehicle becomes disabled for any reason, you'll need to contact your emergency roadside service provider. Before the mechanic or tow truck driver arrives – use a crate or a leash to keep your dog out of the way until the repairs have been made. If work has to be performed inside your RV – keep your dog in a back room or put him in your tow vehicle. Be sure to put a note on the door to let the repairman know there's a dog inside.

Lengthy Repairs

If your recreational vehicle, tow vehicle, or camper requires lengthy repairs while on the road, you may need a plan for dealing with your dog. We have some friends who live in an RV with their two dogs. A couple of years ago, they had to endure several weeks of on-going repairs. Throughout the entire episode, they slept in their RV inside the repair shop each night – while their dogs remained in their car out in the parking lot. As it turned out, the repair shop had a policy restricting pets but not people. It's a lot easier to create a viable back-up plan of your own long before you actually need one.

Fires

Fires represent one of the worst things that can occur in an RV. By the nature of their design, RVs have a tendency to burn intensely while simultaneously releasing toxic chemicals into the air. Consequently, you must design an effective strategy for dealing with a fire before it actually happens.

Make sure that you have plenty of fire extinguishers installed throughout your RV.

For starters, make sure that you have enough smoke detectors. As a practical matter, you should have one in each room of your RV. Also, if one of your smoke detectors goes off all the time, don't remove the battery. Instead, move the detector to a different location. Secondly, install an adequate number of fire extinguishers to handle most situations. Many people keep several extinguishers distributed throughout their vehicle. Likewise, make sure that your extinguishers are capable of putting out a serious fire. If you want to learn more about RV fires, check out **www.macthefireguy.com**. This website is loaded with interesting information and practical advice.

Last but not least, develop an emergency escape plan for getting everyone out in the event of a fire. In our case, we keep several leashes throughout the RV. If we have enough time – we plan to tie the dogs to the nearest tree or a sign post. Setting your dog free should only be considered as a last resort since dogs typically flee from intense situations.

CONDUCT A FIRE DRILL
Perform a fire drill to see if your emergency escape plan will actually work. Remember, the fire may start from the rear of your RV or it could start from the front. Develop a plan for both scenarios. Remember, if extra leashes or pet carriers are normally locked in a storage bin – you won't have enough time to get them in a real fire. Use the drill to flush out these weaknesses.

Traveling with your Dog

Today, nearly half of all campers and RVers routinely bring their dogs with them *(courtesy Philip and Arlene Graham holding Sam and JC).*

The previous chapter (Chapter 4) focused on the planning and preparations that are typically required when camping and RVing with dogs. This chapter, in contrast, deals with life on the road with your dog and other related topics. So whether you're traveling in a motorhome, towing a trailer, driving a truck camper, or living in a tent – this chapter is designed to make your journey easier and safer for you and your dog.

Keeping your Dog Safe and Comfortable

The number one priority, when traveling with dogs, is to

ensure that they're kept safe and comfortable during the entire trip. While this goal may seem obvious to most campers and RVers – there are some people who tend to underestimate the importance of this fundamental principle. As a consequence, thousands of dogs are lost, abandoned, or killed in our country's parks and along our nation's roads – every year. While many of these misfortunes were in all probability unintended, they do suggest the need for a more responsible and caring attitude when traveling and camping with dogs. On that note, the first decision you'll need to make is where to keep your dog during the trip.

Where to Keep your Dog during the Trip

For the most part, you have two basic choices when you go camping and RVing with a dog: keep them in the same vehicle that you'll be traveling in or put them in the vehicle that's being towed (normally a trailer).

Keeping your Dog with you

The most common setup when camping and RVing with dogs is to keep them with you in the same vehicle that you'll be traveling in. With this arrangement – they'll benefit from the same degree of comfort and safety that you enjoy. In addition, you'll be able to keep an eye on your dog in case there's a problem. For example, if one of our dogs starts to whine while we're on the road – we know that its time to pull over and give them a break. On the other hand – if our dogs were kept in a crate inside another vehicle, we wouldn't be aware of their discomfort.

Several years ago, we were traveling across the U.S. and didn't have enough room in the car for all of our pets. As a result, a few of them had to be kept in crates inside the trailer we were towing. Unfortunately, we ended up stopping all the time to make sure that our pets in the trailer were okay. Fortunately, there are now several ways to remotely monitor a dog that's being kept in another vehicle (see below). In any case, if you have the room – it's a lot easier to keep your dog in the same vehicle you'll be in. This is particularly true if you have a motorhome or a bus conversion because of the comfort and the space.

On the other hand, if you're driving a truck or some other passenger vehicle, things can get pretty crowded with a dog. Fortunately, there are a few products on the market that can make your trip safer as well as more convenient for you and your dog. Described in the previous chapter – these pet travel accessories are summarized as follows:

Product	Description
Auxiliary steps	Makes it easier for dogs to enter and exit any vehicle. Particularly useful for smaller dogs and dogs that are physically impaired.
Booster seats	Auxiliary seat improves the view, comfort, and safety of smaller dogs.
Cargo liners	These padded inserts make the rear of a minivan or a SUV more comfortable for your dog.
Non-spill water bowls	Provides dogs with continuous access to drinking water without the risk of spills.

Pet barriers	Fixed or flexible barrier prevents your dog from entering the front of the vehicle. Provides added safety and prevents dogs from barking or lunging at toll booth operators.
Seat covers	Protects original seats from damage, dirt, and pet fur.

Table 1 – Travel-related products for dogs

BUCKLE UP FOR SAFETY

For an added measure of safety, consider using a pet harness that secures your dog to a vehicle's seatbelt. In addition to protecting your dog during a collision, these harnesses provide another crucial benefit in an accident. When medics arrive at an accident scene, they typically open the door of the vehicle to assess the condition of the occupants. When this happens, most dogs jump out of the vehicle and run off – only to become lost or killed by a passing vehicle.

Keeping your Dog in the Towed Vehicle

The second option when camping and RVing with a dog is to keep your dog in a crate inside a towed vehicle such as a travel trailer, fifth wheel, or towed car. People with large dogs or multiple pets often use this approach with considerable success. However, this arrangement has one major drawback: when your dog rides in a towed vehicle – it's harder to adequately monitor and manage their comfort and safety.

Luckily, the next section describes a few products that can help in this regard.

Monitoring your Dogs Remotely

One of the easiest ways to keep an eye on a dog that's being kept in a towed vehicle is to install a baby monitor. Inexpensive and readily available, baby monitors will enable you to monitor your dog from virtually any vehicle. Some models only provide listening capabilities while others have a built-in camera so you can actually see your dog. To simplify the installation, look for a baby monitor that can operate on batteries. Otherwise, you'll have to use an inverter.

If your dog travels in a trailer — you'll need some way to make sure they're safe.

If you prefer a more sophisticated solution, consider a remote video monitoring system. These high-tech devices enable you to observe any environment you want with the help of a remote camera and a wireless transceiver. In addition, the cameras that come with these systems are often fitted with special lenses that provide a wide angle view in low-light settings – perfect for a towed vehicle. Some of these systems come with multiple cameras to provide different views of your trailer's interior. Remote video monitoring systems are less expensive than you might think and can be found in consumer electronics stores and of course, on the Internet.

Using a Crate

When keeping a dog in a towed vehicle, they must always be kept in a cage or a pet crate. Crates provide a number of benefits including keeping your dog safely contained, reducing the possibility of something falling on them, and ensuring there are no fights (when traveling with multiple dogs). You can find dog crates of all sizes in most pet stores. Nearly all crates come with a hinged metal door and tamper-proof latches. Some even have slide-out trays to facilitate cleaning. However, this feature is more appropriate for birds than dogs.

Most crates are made of molded plastic or heavy welded steel wire. The plastic ones are typically two-piece units with ventilation slots along the sides and a welded steel wire door in the front. Plastic crates are lightweight, highly portable, and can be taken apart for storage. When shopping for a plastic crate – look for one that's big enough for comfort and sturdy enough to resist serious chewing.

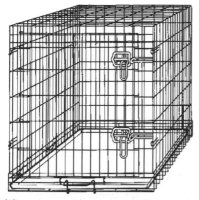

Steel wire crates are also very popular and depending on your needs, may be a better choice than plastic. While steel wire crates aren't normally approved for airline use – they do provide better ventilation for your dog. In addition, it's virtually impossible to chew through a steel wire crate. However, pay close attention when purchasing a wire crate because there is a wide variability in product quality. Some are flimsy and cannot be broken down for storage. Others are advertised as "collapsible" but do so only with considerable difficulty. Look for sturdy models that are easily folded up for convenient storage.

Wire crates provide superior ventilation and are usually collapsible for easy storage.

DOG CRATE COMMANDMENTS

Never leave a dog in a crate for more than two hours at a time. That way, you'll be able to intervene if there's a problem (i.e. the air conditioner has stopped working). In addition, since crates are physically confining – take your dog out for a walk several times a day. Likewise, don't make your dog urinate or defecate in their crate. Take them outside for this purpose and praise them whenever they leave or enter the crate. If your dog exhibits signs of stress when they're in the crate – take them out at once. Your dog's crate should always be seen as a safe, comfortable, and clean environment. It should never become a symbol of suffering or punishment.

Securing the Crate

If you do use a crate, you'll need to secure it to the floor of the trailer to keep it from moving around. Most people use ratchet tie-downs and floor cleats. The tie-downs are available at discount and hardware stores. Fold-down cleats are generally found at auto parts stores, marine supply outlets, and on the Internet. Alternatively, you can also install mounting rings on the walls of your trailer. In any case, make sure the cleats or the mounting rings are attached securely. U.S. Cargo Control (**www.uscargocontrol.com**) has an impressive selection of cargo security hardware.

Keeping them Cool

If you do plan to keep your dog in a crate – make sure there's plenty of fresh air, a source of clean water, and a comfortable place for your dog to sleep. It should also be tall enough for your dog to stand up. In addition, experienced pet haulers always use crates that are large enough to accommodate a foam pad for sleeping and a spill-proof water bowl. At the same time, you'll need to ensure that your dog has plenty of fresh air and is kept cool during warm weather. To bring fresh air into the towed vehicle, install a thermostatically controlled roof vent. That way, if the vehicle gets too warm – the vent will automatically open and the fan will turn on.

Also, consider installing a pet crate cooling fan. These battery-operated fans attach to any crate and will help to keep your dog comfortable and safe from excess heat while on the road. If you don't have a reliable way to keep your dog cool, forget about keeping them inside a towed vehicle. On a sunny day, the temperature inside a trailer can become dangerously high in less time than you think. Likewise, if the weather becomes hot and the air conditioner in your towed vehicle breaks down – you're going to have to find some way to keep your dog cool. That's why it's crucial to check up on your dog as often as possible.

KEEP YOUR DOG IN THE FRONT
Most trailers have very simple suspension systems that tend to deliver a surprisingly harsh ride. Therefore, if you plan on keeping your dog in a trailer, place the crate as far to the front (near the hitch) as possible. The further back you go in a towed vehicle, the harsher the ride. Also, consider placing the crate on a piece of foam. It will dampen some of the vibration and soften the bumps.

═Traveling with Multiple Dogs═

As full-time RVers, we occasionally meet other RVers who are transporting animals to a dog show. In some cases, they are traveling with as many as a dozen dogs in a single vehicle. While this may sound impracticable on its face, it's surprising how well these folks handle all these dogs. As you'll see from the following observations – safety is a very high priority:

 Toy haulers have become very popular with campers and RVers that transport large groups of dogs. These specialized RVs include large open areas that are easily accessible via wide entranceways and drop-down ramps. In addition, toy-hauler floors are extremely durable and include built-in floor cleats and tie-down rings that are perfect for securing pet cages or crates. The front of the toy hauler is usually configured like a conventional RV.

🐾 In addition to relying on roof fans and air conditioners, each crate has its own battery-operated fan to keep the air circulating.

🐾 Every crate is secured with heavy strapping that is attached to secure floor cleats and wall rings.

🐾 Some RVers use web cams, baby monitors, walkie talkies, or camera-based surveillance systems to monitor their dogs. These video monitoring systems often include audio capabilities so the driver can hear as well as see the dogs.

🐾 Smoke, propane, and carbon monoxide detectors are crucial to ensure that the dogs are safe at all times. While the smoke and carbon monoxide detectors are installed on the ceiling, propane detectors are always installed at the floor level since propane is heavier than air. Correspondingly, several fire extinguishers are placed in convenient locations. Batteries are replaced every 90 days.

🐾 People that routinely transport large groups of dogs perform regular fire drills. As a result – they already know exactly what to do if a fire breaks out.

🐾 The dogs are given water throughout the trip. Similarly, they are let out of their crates for a walk at one hundred mile intervals.

🐾 The medical records for each dog are typically

secured to their cage with the help of bungee cords.

🐾 The driver always brings a listing of emergency animal hospitals in each state. Thus, if a dog becomes ill or is injured – they can quickly locate and head for the nearest facility.

🐾 A laptop with wireless Internet access keeps the drivers informed of changing weather conditions, travel advisories, and other important matters. GPS systems are also extensively used.

🐾 Backup AC generators are frequently employed to provide power (for air conditioning) in case the vehicle becomes too warm.

🐾 RVers that transport large groups of dogs utilize various solutions for keeping their dogs safely contained while at campgrounds. For a detailed discussion of available containment options – please refer to Chapter 7.

The rear of this camper van has been modified to safely transport several dogs.

As expected, RVs are used extensively by show dog professionals and other people who travel with groups of dogs. Many, in fact, remove the furniture from their RVs in order to make room for pet cages. However, before you decide to do the same – read the following advice:

BE CAREFUL WHEN REMODELING YOUR RV FOR DOGS
When traveling with groups of dogs, many campers and RVers modify their vehicle in order to make room for pet crates. In a motorhome, the sofa or the dinette is often removed for this purpose. Since most motorhomes are typically built like houses on a chassis, this strategy will work fine. However, if you plan on removing built-in furniture in a trailer, be careful. Trailers can be tricky in terms of structural integrity. One person removed a bunk bed only to find out that the bed was part of the trailer's supporting infrastructure. When they started installing the pet crates, the trailer's slide-out began to collapse. Consequently, if you plan to modify a trailer to accommodate pet cages – first contact the manufacturer to make sure that your plans can be safely implemented.

Traveling with Puppies

Camping and RVing with young dogs and puppies is a challenging proposition but it can be done with some careful planning and a lot of patience. Following are a few suggestions:

Most puppies aren't housebroken. As a result, when you're traveling, you'll need to stop more often to let them do their business. Even so, bring a lot of paper towels.

Possibly because they are more secure – crate trained puppies tend to do well when traveling (if they're kept in their crate). However, they'll need to be taken out of their crates frequently.

Puppies rarely obey commands. Consequently, they should be kept on a leash at all times. In addition, make sure their collars are snug (just enough room for two fingers). Plump little puppies have a tendency to slip out of their collars. For containment strategies while staying at a campground, please refer to Chapter 7.

Even though they're puppies, make sure they are wearing ID tags just in case.

Puppies are highly susceptible to motion sickness. Therefore, avoid feeding them before you leave and consider keeping them in a crate while you're on the road.

Don't switch foods when traveling with puppies. They have undeveloped intestinal tracts that tend to react badly to sudden dietary changes.

Make sure that your RV is "puppy-proof". Pay close attention to stored chemicals, seat belts, small objects, electrical cords, and furniture legs.

🐾 If possible, bring the mother. She'll look after the puppies and handle any disciplinary issues.

Camping and RVing with a puppy requires a lot of patience and plenty of love.

══Camping and RVing with══ Mixed Pets

Many campers and RVers wonder if it's possible to travel with other animals in addition to dogs. Besides plenty of cats, we've seen campers (with dogs) traveling with guinea pigs, birds, lizards, snakes, hamsters, fish, and even goats. Provided each creature is properly secured and adequately cared for, anything is possible. Key issues tend to be sufficient heating, ventilating and cooling, animal safety, food and water, and routine maintenance.

Campers and RVers routinely travel with a wide assortment of pets.

As expected, full-time RVers tend to travel with the greatest variety of animals. As a result, they often develop creative solutions to accommodate their guests. Every so often, we'll encounter a motorhome with hanging bird cages, elaborate cat walks, built-in reptile cages, and other ingenious solutions. While some people might shudder at the thought – I think it would be interesting to travel with different creatures.

Traveling with Dogs and Children

As full-time RVers, we've traveled with dogs, cats, and more recently, a baby girl. Simply put, camping and RVing with dogs and children is fundamentally the same. Attend to their needs, make safety the topmost priority, and have fun.

When things seem out of hand and overwhelming, don't forget, you'll probably look back to these crazy times and wish you could do it all again. In any case, here are a few tips for the road if your plans involve camping and RVing with dogs and kids:

- While on the road, involve the children in the daily care of your dog. This might include feeding, brushing, and taking the dog for a walk. It will help the children to develop a sense of responsibility and kindness.

- Keep the children away from the dog's food, toys, and sleeping area. In an RV, space is at a premium. If your dog feels crowded and pressured – he may get frustrated and lash out at the kids.

- Young children often let dogs run free. Teach the kids to put the dog on a leash before leaving the RV.

That way, there's no chance that your dog will get hurt or lost while on the road.

Crossing the U.S. Border with Your Dog

Even if you don't have any plans to travel into Canada or Mexico, it always pays to be prepared. We've met travelers who have decided on a whim to join an RV caravan that was going down to Mexico. Fortunately, with a little planning, it's easy to prepare for a border crossing with a dog. The regulations described in this section are subject to change so be sure to confirm these requirements before you go.

The Canadian Border

You can take a dog into Canada if you have a valid rabies vaccination certificate signed by a licensed veterinarian. The certificate must identify the dog's breed, color, sex, and weight. It should also indicate the trade name of the vaccine used; the serial number; the vaccination date; and the duration of validity. If a validity date doesn't appear on the certificate – it will automatically be considered a one-year vaccine. If you don't have a rabies certificate, an inspector will require you to have your dog vaccinated before you can cross into Canada.

Special Purpose Dogs

Assistance dogs that are certified as a guide, hearing, seizure, or other service dog, are not subject to any importation restrictions if the person traveling with the dog is the owner and accompanies the dog into Canada.

The Mexican Border

Both Mexico and the U.S. enforce rather stringent regulations about pets. That being said, many people routinely bring their dogs across the Mexican border without any problems or any formalities. For dogs taken into Mexico and returned to the United States – owners must present an International Health Certificate (form 77-043) signed by a licensed veterinarian. The certificate will be stamped at the border or at the Mexican consulate (where tourist cards are obtained). The certificate should be issued no more than 72 hours before the animal enters Mexico. The rabies vaccination certificate must be dated no earlier than one month nor later than twelve months (from the current date).

Stopping to Give Your Dog a Break

No matter where you keep your dog while traveling, you must still take them for a walk every few hours. This will provide you with a break as well.

Although walking a dog is pretty straightforward, there are a few things to keep in mind:

Walk them when you have the chance	Life on the road can often be unpredictable. Rest stops are frequently closed for repairs and highways are sometimes detoured towards unknown roads and unfamiliar towns. In addition, it's often impossible to pull an RV onto the breakdown lane of a crowded highway. Therefore, if you see a good place to walk your dog – pull over. It might be a while before you have another chance.
Be careful when you pull over	When you stop to walk your dog, be careful where you pull over. RVs and campers can take up a lot of room. There's a true story about a couple that created a three hour backup on the New Jersey Turnpike when they blocked a lane

Give yourself a lot of room and plenty of time to pull out.

in order to take their dog for a walk on the highway's center strip.

When you do pull over, choose a level stretch of highway that has good visibility from both directions. Also, put your emergency flashers on. That way, you'll be seen by others and you'll have adequate visibility when you're ready to pull back on the road.

Don't let your dog get loose	You need to make sure that your dog never gets loose while you're on the road. Since they're in unfamiliar territory, dogs are unable to figure out where they are. One proven trick is to put their leash on before you open the door to your vehicle. If you do get separated from your dog, please refer to Chapter 7.
Watch out for Trucks	When you're at a rest stop, you may be required to park your RV with the big rigs. When you go out to walk your dog, make sure that the truck next to you isn't ready to pull out. In addition, some dogs get startled by the sound of diesel engines and air brakes. As a result, keep a tight grip on their leash.
When you leave, crack the windows and lock the doors	When you go to the restroom or grab a bite to eat at a rest area – be sure to crack the windows and lock the doors. A woman in South Carolina recently had two show dogs stolen from her

vehicle when she forgot to lock the car. Fortunately, the dogs were later returned (under highly questionable circumstances).

| **Pick up after your dog** | Whenever you stop at a rest area, pick up after your dog. If you don't – you're effectively leaving it for others to clean up (or step in). |

This retractable leash is fitted with a small saddlebag that can hold plenty of pet clean-up bags (shown).

| **Park in the shade to keep your dog cool** | At rest stops, try to park in the shade. If there aren't any trees, park next to a building. During the summer, always use a reflective windshield screen to reduce the effects of the sun. |

Give your dog lots of fresh water	Give your dog an opportunity to drink water whenever possible. Keep a spare bowl and a jug of water in your vehicle. For some reason – traveling seems to make dogs thirsty.
Prepare for wet weather	In rainy weather, keep a towel nearby to dry off your dog. Also, place an umbrella near the door for walks in the rain. You can even purchase disposable plastic booties that will keep your dog's feet dry and your vehicle's carpet clean.

Finding Places to Stay with a Dog

The key to camping and RVing with a dog is to find a campground that's perfect for you.

This chapter focuses on the issue of locating an acceptable place to stay while camping and RVing with a dog. While most parks and campgrounds accept dogs – there's often more to the picture than meets the eye. For example, countless parks and campgrounds impose discriminatory pet policies that effectively prohibit many of the most popular dog breeds. In the same way, numerous campgrounds are so crowded and poorly planned – it's virtually impossible to stay there with a dog without experiencing major problems. Consequently, it's not always as simple as it should be to locate a campground that's truly suitable for people with dogs.

Fortunately, this chapter describes several proven ways to identify as well as evaluate pets-welcome campgrounds. As a result, by the time you're done reading this chapter – you'll have no trouble finding places that are perfect for both of you.

CAMPGROUND SURFING
The Internet is turning out to be one of the best sources of first-hand information about camping. With the advent of blogs and online forums – you can spend hours reading about other people's experiences at various parks and campgrounds. To begin, type in the name of a park you're interested in and see what shows up.

Types of Campgrounds

As a camper or RVer with a dog, you have a wide range of options in terms of where to "pitch your tent". Best of all, there's an amazing variety of parks and campgrounds in North America. While most of these places do accept dogs – there are significant differences depending on the type of campground you end up staying at. Today, the vast majority of parks and campgrounds typically fall into one of the following classifications:

Private Campgrounds and RV Parks ~ Representing the largest group of parks and campgrounds in North America, privately owned facilities make up the vast majority of listings that are included in most campground directories.

RV Resorts ~ The title "RV resort" is simply a marketing term that describes a growing collection of privately owned RV parks. In reality, RV resorts range from small campgrounds with basic amenities to luxurious RV communities with swimming pools, golf courses, tennis courts, local entertainment, and a non-stop litany of activities.

Public Campgrounds and RV Parks – This group includes a broad selection of municipal, county, and regional parks and campgrounds. Public campgrounds are typically well run, conveniently located, and reasonably priced.

State Parks – These parks are owned and operated by state agencies. Normally located within naturally attractive settings – state parks are frequently in close proximity to recreational areas, bodies of water, and conservation districts.

State parks tend to offer fantastic scenery, pristine lakes, and lots of recreation.

National Parks and Federal Recreational Lands –
These parks, run by the National Forest Service or
the National Park Service, are located within large
well-preserved tracts of land that have been put aside
for recreational and conservation purposes. They
generally offer natural beauty, spacious campsites,
and plenty of hiking.

Public Lands – The majority of public lands in the
U.S. are held in trust for the American people by the
federal government. They are customarily managed
by the Bureau of Land Management, the United States
National Park Service, and other federal agencies.
Public lands are often isolated, rugged, and beautiful.

Choosing the Type of Campground to Stay At

With respect to camping or RVing with a dog, each type
of facility listed above has various advantages as well as a
few drawbacks. As a practical matter – your choice should
ultimately depend on your camping objectives as well
as your personal preferences. Here are some tips when
choosing the type of campground:

Convenience and Close Proximity to Area Interests

If your top priorities are convenience and close proximity
to your destination – grab your campground directory and

pick one of the private campgrounds in the area. The reason is simple. They usually have full hook-ups and there are so many private campgrounds – it's easy to find one close to your destination. While these campgrounds are often crowded and relatively inconvenient for dog owners – they're a good option for people who are looking for a convenient place to stay for a few nights. Pricing is generally based on the location and the campground's proximity to popular tourist attractions.

National parks deliver world-class beauty and bargain prices for many Americans.

Convenient Location and Greater Privacy

If you're looking for a balanced blend of scenic beauty, reasonable rates, and convenient location, check out the publically owned parks and campgrounds in the area. They are normally less expensive than private parks and usually provide greater site privacy and more breathing room for dog owners. On the downside, they usually have dump stations as opposed to individual sewer hook-ups. They also tend to be a little more primitive than some private campgrounds. But for people who are looking for a more natural setting for themselves as well as their dog – publically owned parks and campgrounds are a good compromise.

Relatively Good Location and Natural Beauty

If your primary goal is to immerse yourself in everything natural but you don't want to drive forever to get there, head for the nearest state or federal park. These facilities are normally located in beautiful settings and as a result – are perfect for getting away from it all. Woodsy, primitive, and casual, state parks rarely have hookups with the possible exception of water. However, many have dump stations and public water supplies. For dog owners – this is practically as good as it gets.

STATE PARKS HAVE SOME OF THE BEST WATER
While some campgrounds and RV parks have swimming pools, this doesn't do much for your dog. If your dog truly loves to swim — check out the state and federal parks. Many have lakes and some even have campsites right on the shore!

Breathtaking Natural Beauty and Abundant Wildlife

If you're looking for the ultimate camping experience, make a reservation at a national park. Examples include: Yosemite,

Yellowstone, Acadia, and Bryce Canyon. The downside to national parks includes crowds, bears, and traffic. The advantages are too numerous to list. However, before you go, refer to Chapter 8 (dealing with bears). If you're 62 or over, or permanently disabled – you can get a pass that offers substantial discounts. They also have annual passes for frequent visitors. Go to the National Park Service website (**www.nps.gov**) for details.

Negligible Cost and Rugged Natural Beauty

If you're idea of the ultimate camping trip includes off-the-grid living and rugged surroundings – check out the nation's public lands. Bargain priced and lacking in most amenities, public lands are the perfect place to disappear. We've stayed

The nation's public lands offer rugged beauty, plenty of privacy, and few conveniences.

on public lands in western Arizona and didn't see another human being for weeks. The wind never stopped blowing and the landscape was craggy and intense. It wouldn't have surprised anyone if a dinosaur showed up.

As for our dogs, they felt like they had gone back in time. Without the need for leashes, they ran and played for hours. When the sun went down, they sat around a crackling fire under a star-lit sky listening to their kindred coyotes howling at the moon. We did occasionally have to lug water and find a place to empty our tanks – but that didn't seem to matter at the time.

The point here is that when it comes to camping and RVing with dogs – the type of park can make a big difference. In general, the scale runs the full gamut from luxurious RV communities in big cities to primitive campgrounds a hundred miles from nowhere. For dog owners, the choice is a matter of style. In our case, we prefer campgrounds that are less crowded and more natural than your typical RV park. Our dogs have the opportunity to explore nature at its best and we get a chance to experience the finest camping on the planet. While the consequences are usually fewer conveniences – we usually think it's a trade-off that's well worth the price.

How to Use a Campground Directory

With respect to finding a campground, we've concluded that Woodall's campground directories are more comprehensive and easier to use than other competing directories.

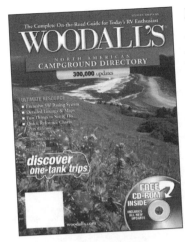

For example, Woodall's North American Campground Directory provides quick-reference charts at the beginning of each state to simplify the process of finding pet-welcome campgrounds. The North American edition also includes an interactive CD-ROM (Mac & PC compatible) that enables you to easily search for RV campgrounds, RV Dealers & Service Centers and interesting things to see and do on your computer or laptop. The CD-ROM contains all the same information as the directory and you don't need an Internet connection to use it. Plus, it comes with some

With The Woodall's North American Campground Directory, it's easy to find a pet-welcome campground *(courtesy Ken and Ildi Waller with their Schipperke, Kormi)*.

pretty entertaining children's activities to keep the kids or grandkids busy and a few handy RV checklists. Best of all, it's completely FREE with the purchase of the directory.

With regards to dogs, each directory listing includes some information about their pet policy. If the listing reads

"No Pets", it means that the park doesn't allow dogs of any kind. If the listing reads "Pet Restrictions", it means that the campground accepts some dogs. Since this designation is somewhat vague – always call ahead to determine their actual pet policy. ($) indicates that a fee is imposed for dogs. The guides also suggest that if you're traveling with a large or unusual dog, or with several dogs – call the campground to see if your dog(s) will be accepted.

Pet-Related Policies and Restrictions

It should be an easy matter to figure out which campgrounds accept dogs and which don't. However, as a practical matter, this task can be surprisingly complicated because of the way most campgrounds depict their policy towards dogs. Since few campgrounds want to turn away potential customers – they rarely state outright that they don't accept dogs. Instead, some campgrounds effectively limit the presence of dogs by using subjective criteria such as the dog's weight or breed, or the number of dogs you have. As a result, most dog owners are unable to determine a campground's actual policy towards dogs until they actually register. On that note, when you're looking for a campground – here are some things to keep in mind:

Keep high standards	Places that are genuinely dog-friendly are a pleasure to stay at. They appreciate what it's like to travel and camp with dogs and best of all, they sincerely enjoy animals. When you find a place like this – you'll know it.

Talk to other dog owners	Talk to other RVers and campers with dogs. They're a great source of information regarding pets-welcome (or pets-unwelcome) campgrounds.
Call before you go	Even if a campground advertises that it's pets-welcome, call them before you arrive. That way – you'll be able to verify that your dog will actually be accepted when you arrive.
Look for sensible pet policies	Places that are truly dog-friendly normally have straightforward pet policies. A typical example of a reasonable policy reads: "All dogs must be on a leash and owners are required to pick up after their dogs." Simple and reasonable.

In the real world, dogs come in all sizes and breeds *(courtesy Debbie Echols and Alan McFadden).*

Avoid arbitrary pet restrictions	Campgrounds that have size restrictions (i.e. nothing over 25 lbs) or limits on the number of pets you can bring, are not really pets-welcome. Dogs come in all sizes and quantities. If you want to stay at a campground that genuinely welcomes all dogs – avoid places with discriminatory pet policies.
Be leery of pet fees	In our opinion, campgrounds that charge an extra fee for dogs have simply found another way to increase their profits. After all, most pets-welcome campgrounds seem to do just fine without charging an extra fee.
Be aware of unrealistic pet rules	Some campgrounds have a rule that states that you cannot leave a dog unattended. However, in truth, many campers leave their dogs alone in their RV without causing any problems (see Chapter 7 for details). Fortunately for dog owners, this rule is rarely enforced.
Scrutinize breed restrictions	There are very few dog breeds that can be considered inherently dangerous. We understand the emotion behind banning certain breeds. However, the vast majority of campgrounds somehow get by without these restrictions.

Finding a Pets-welcome Campground

Even if a campground states they are "pets-welcome", there are other considerations that can impact the facility's suitability for dogs. In other words, while designated pet policies are important – other factors may actually play a bigger role in determining whether or not the campground is appropriate for dogs. Here are a few tips to help you identify parks and campgrounds that are truly pets-welcome.

Avoid crowded campgrounds	Some campgrounds are small, tightly packed, and short on privacy. Places like these can be stressful for dogs as well as their owners. Before registering, try to get some idea of the campground's layout and the level of privacy at each site. In some parks, it's almost impossible to walk your dog without stepping on someone else's site. If you have the choice – avoid places like these.
Watch out for pet-unfriendly residents	We stayed at a campground that indicated it welcomed pets. However, when we took our dogs for a walk, we were met with negative comments and disapproving stares. If a park has a pet policy that the residents don't support – it might as well prohibit all dogs.

Look around	When you first get to a campground, take a close look around. If you see other dogs running free and evidence that pet owners aren't picking up after their dogs – get ready to leave in the morning. Pet rules are for everyone's benefit.
Consider state parks	State parks and campgrounds tend to be less crowded than privately owned ones. They also tend to be more casual towards dogs. However, many publicly owned parks lack the full hookups and extra services that are often available at privately owned campgrounds.

State parks tend to offer more room for people and their dogs.

Check out the reviews	There's a website (**www.rvparkreviews. com**) that posts reviews and comments about specific campgrounds. While some of the reviews may lack objectivity – they can be interesting as well as helpful.
Don't judge a book by its cover	Don't pay too much attention to photos in a brochure or on a website. The photos are usually designed to make the facility look better than it really is. Conversely, some RV parks and campgrounds seem very crowded in their ads. But in reality, they might be a great place to stay because of the size of each site or the actual degree of site privacy.
Ask about isolated sites	When you first arrive at a campground, ask if there are any sites that offer more privacy than others. It's always easier with dogs when you have a little extra breathing room. We also look for sites that aren't close to restrooms, playgrounds, and other high-traffic areas.
Assess their pet provisions	The best pets-welcome campgrounds have special provisions for dogs such as walking trails, planned activities, and dedicated play areas. When you're calling a campground, ask if they have any special provisions. It will also give you an opportunity to get a feel for their attitude towards dogs.

This campground has a special pet playground where dogs can run free without a leash.

Trust your instincts	If after talking to a campground host, you get the distinct feeling that they don't like dogs – go somewhere else. There are plenty of campgrounds that genuinely enjoy pets.
Talk to other dog owners	If you have the opportunity – talk to other campers and RVers with dogs. They may be able to provide you with some valuable insight into the campground's true policy regarding dogs.
Keep an open mind	Sometimes, unsuitable campgrounds can be acceptable in the short run if there are mitigating factors. We once pulled into a campground in Las Vegas that was unusually crowded with virtually no

site privacy. However, as it turned out, the campground was convenient to the strip, had full hookups, and was adjacent to a large public park that was perfect for walking the dogs. It was also full of interesting people.

Boondocking with Dogs

Boondocking essentially means spending the night in a location that is not a designated park or campground. Popular boondocking locations include Wal-Mart parking lots, Flying J truck stops, public streets, back roads, fields, highway rest stops, and beaches. We've had to boondock a number of times when traveling through regions of the country that don't have any campgrounds that are open. Examples include much of the Northeast between the months of November and May.

Boondocking is also an effective way to get by if you're financially strapped for cash. While some people believe that boondocking isn't fair to campground owners – there are situations when there's no alternative. As full-time RVers, we know what its like to be driving at night with no place to stop. In this situation, boondocking is both a reasonable solution as well as an American tradition. In any case – here are a few suggestions when boondocking with a dog:

Be careful where you park your RV

When you pull into a deserted area late at night, it's hard to see all of the features. On one occasion, we unknowingly parked next to a train track. At two in the morning, we discovered our mistake. Likewise, we once stayed in a place where other truckers spent the night. By morning, we were worn out from the non-stop noise of the diesel engines and the refrigerator trucks.

Don't walk your dog late at night	One of the advantages of a campground is the fact that they provide a certain degree of security. However, when you're spending the night in a parking lot – there are no guarantees. Consequently, try to walk your dog earlier in the evening and avoid places that feel unsafe.
If you plan on staying in a Wal-Mart, call ahead	We always call each Wal-Mart before we arrive and ask if it's okay to spend the night in their parking lot. That way, you can make sure that you're not violating any rules. In some cases, they'll even tell you where to park. Bear in mind – RVers are some of their best customers.
Be a good neighbor	If you notice another RVer who's having a problem – see if there's anything you can do to help. At a minimum, be friendly and acknowledge their existence. After all – you may be the one that needs help the next time.

Keep a low profile	There are three principal rules to boondocking. 1) Don't spend more than one night; 2) Don't block anyone in or out and; 3) Try to remain inconspicuous. For example, if you pull into a Wal-Mart parking lot, roll out your awning, and have an outdoor picnic with live music – you're probably pushing your luck.
Let your dog bark	Dogs are extremely effective deterrents of crime. The reason has to do with the fact that most criminals want to be unobtrusive when breaking the law. A barking dog is the last thing they want to deal with. When your dog starts to bark for no apparent reason – don't stop him. He has better hearing than you and he's simply doing his job.
Stay alert and be prepared to leave	Occasionally, we've stayed in places that turn out to be unacceptable for various reasons. Make sure you can leave quickly if you have to.

Fortunately, there are many places and lots of ways to camp and RV with a dog. As with most things in life – common sense can go a long way. As for us, we can't imagine camping without a dog. There are so many advantages and so few drawbacks. The next chapter deals with life at the campground with a dog. Hence, it's one of the book's most important chapters.

Campground Life with a Dog

With this campground setup, Chuka and Wolf-2
have it made in the shade *(courtesy Doug Noyce
and Barbara Gold)*.

In spite of the fact that most campgrounds claim they are
pets-welcome, many of the difficulties that affect campers
and RVers with dogs occur while staying at RV parks and
campgrounds.

Accordingly, this chapter focuses on the numerous issues
that campers and RVers with dogs typically tackle at most
campgrounds. It begins with what to do when you first get to
a campground and then explores ways to keep your dog safe,
entertained, and out of trouble. It goes on to describe how to
take pictures of your dog, what steps to take if your dog gets
lost, and the advantages and drawbacks of being a work camper
with a dog. For these reasons – this is an important chapter.

═ Pets-Welcome Campgrounds ═

While most RV parks and campgrounds consider themselves to be "pets-welcome"– you may be surprised at the wide range of attitudes, policies, and behaviors that you come across as a dog owner. Some of the unpredictability is understandable. After all, even though nearly half of all campers and RVers bring dogs, an equal or greater number do not. Thus, while we may think that dogs are indeed man's best friend – there are plenty of others that prefer the company of people rather than dogs. As full-time RVers who have always traveled with dogs, we know that even though a campground may state that it's pets-welcome – it doesn't mean that everyone that stays there is.

═ Arriving at the Campground ═

Whether you're staying at a campground for a single night or spending an entire season, there are a few things that you should do before you arrive. First, try to call the campground to verify that your dog is in fact accepted. As described earlier, pets-welcome campgrounds aren't necessarily friendly to all dogs.

In addition, some campgrounds appear to have discretionary rules regarding dogs. On a recent trip to Florida, we had a difficult time finding a campground that would accept our two German Shepherd dogs. In some instances, the campground would state on the phone that our dogs would be fine. But when we arrived, we were told that only small dogs were allowed. Hence, when you call a campground to verify their pet policy – get the name of the person you're speaking with.

Even though our dogs are completely trained – it isn't always easy to find a campground.

Second, unruly dogs tend to make campground owners nervous. If you have a dog that becomes overexcited whenever they get to a new place – find some way to calm them down while you sign in. If that strategy fails, have someone take them for a walk while you register. We aren't suggesting that you sneak your dog in. We're simply describing a way to make the registration process a little less hectic. On the other hand, if a campground host makes a disparaging remark about your dog, consider going somewhere else. There are plenty of campgrounds that genuinely welcome campers with real dogs.

VACCINATION RECORDS

When camping and RVing with a dog, be sure to keep a copy of your dog's vaccination records in a convenient location in case it's required to register. The document should clearly indicate that your dog is up-to-date on their rabies shots. Chapter 9 includes a pet health record form that will enable you to keep a record of your dog's vaccination history.

When you first pull into your campsite, take your dog for a quick walk. Then give them some water. Besides quenching their thirst, this simple gesture will let them know that this place is going to be their temporary home for a while. Even though our dogs have stayed at hundreds of campgrounds, they still won't settle down until we've taken them for a quick walk.

Whenever they arrive at a new campground – Robert always takes Scrappy for a quick walk to check things out *(courtesy Robert Heinz)*.

Lining up Emergency Medical Care

Two years ago, while staying at a campground in the Southwest, I thought I was having a heart attack. As a result, I called 911 and within minutes, two trained medics arrived in an ambulance. In contrast, if you have an emergency regarding your dog – there's no one to call. In this scenario, saving your dog's life will be your responsibility.

Venomous snakes are common in much of North America.

Luckily, there is an effective way to prepare for an emergency like this. Using the yellow pages or the Internet – get the address and phone number of the nearest emergency animal hospital. The campground owners might also be able to tell you where it is. At any rate, make sure that the facility is open seven days a week, 24 hours a day. After that, purchase a map and use a marker (or a highlighter) to show the precise location of the hospital

WITH A SNAKEBITE – EVERY MINUTE COUNTS
Each year, more than fifteen thousand dogs are bitten by venomous snakes. If your dog is one of them – you have around thirty minutes to get them treated with the correct antivenin. If you already know where to bring them, you'll save precious amounts of time. Try to describe the snake but don't make any attempt to kill it or capture it (to bring it in). Otherwise – you could become the next victim.

in relationship to the campground. When you're finished, put the marked-up map in your vehicle. Then, if your dog requires emergency medical care, you'll know exactly where to go. Last but not least – be sure to call the animal hospital while on the way so they can take steps to prepare for your arrival.

Caring for Your Dog When You Can't

If you leave your dog alone at the campground for any reason, there could be a serious problem (with your dog) if something were to happen to you. Fortunately, there's an easy way to protect your pets in this scenario. Simply fill out two identical index cards like the example shown below. Place one card in your wallet or your purse and another in your vehicle (where someone can easily find it).

My name is Bob Smith. I'm currently staying at site # 127 in the Big Valley Campground in Springdale, Virginia. There's one dog (Max) and one cat (Pudge) in the motorhome. If you find this note, please call the campground (302-555-6208) to make sure that someone cares for my two pets. My cell phone number is 417-555-1673. If you can't get through, please call my wife Jan at 417-555-0122 or my brother Ray at 417-555-0488 (rsmith@hotmail.com). My vet is Dr. Alan Shipman at 417-555-8630. Thank you for your help!

A note like this can eliminate the possibility of your pets being abandoned if something were to happen to you. Put one copy in your car and keep another on your person.

Securing Your Dog at a Campground

There are two good reasons for keeping your dog contained while staying at a campground. Firstly, it's the rule. Secondly, your dog can't get lost if he's properly secured. This second point might seem a little excessive but you would be surprised at how many dogs are lost each year at campgrounds. The first time we saw someone lose their dog, we thought is was highly unusual. But when we became work campers and got to know the local rangers, we discovered, to our horror, that campers and RVers lose their dogs all the time. Worst of all – most are never found. The circumstances vary but one fact is always the same – the dogs weren't adequately secured.

Portable pet pens are one of the best ways to keep dogs safely contained at a campground
(courtesy Ginny and Harry Bufkin with Star, Bogey, Rugby, and Abbey).

When you first get to a campground, you'll need to find some way to keep your dog contained within your campsite. Fortunately, there are several effective methods for securing your dog. We've seen everything from simple pieces of rope to chain-link kennels with elaborate roofing. The following table summarizes the most commonly used containment solutions.

Table 1 – Portable Options for Securing Dogs at a Campsite

Method	Benefits	Drawbacks
Chain, coated metal cable, or rope	Can be secured to any stationary object. **NOTE:** Regular chain will rust and stain surfaces and hands. Always use stainless steel chain.	Unlike chain, coated cable has a tendency to get caught up in a dog's legs. Rope can be chewed by most dogs. Some dogs are prone to accidental strangulation. No protection from rain and insects.
Dog runs	Provides good mobility and minimizes tangling.	Requires adequate room and a place to secure the run. Most campgrounds prohibit securing anything to trees. Some dogs are prone to accidental strangulation. No protection from rain and insects.
Portable pet fencing (i.e. ExPen™)	Expandable and easy to set up. Relatively secure (for most dogs). Roomy.	Requires dedicated storage. Fencing must be tall enough and secured to the ground to keep dogs contained.
Crates and pet cages	Easy to set up. Extremely secure for all dogs.	Requires dedicated storage. Poor air circulation. Confining. No protection from rain and insects.

Chain-link fencing	Extremely secure and expandable. Can easily support a roof. Roomy.	Requires dedicated storage. Heavy, bulky. No protection from rain and insects.
Screen rooms (free standing or attached to RV awning)	No sun, bugs, or rain. Provides living space for people and dogs. Folds up for convenient storage. Relatively light weight.	Requires dedicated storage. Must be secured to the ground. Models attached to awning may have to be taken down in high winds. Some dogs will be able to break through the screening.
Combo System (i.e. a portable pet fencing unit inside a small screen house).	Secure. Roomy. Provides protection from sun, rain, and insects. Easy to set up. Very portable.	Requires dedicated storage. Fencing must be tall enough and secured to the ground to keep dogs contained.

CAMPGROUND CONTAINMENT SAFETY RULES
If you keep your dog secured outside, make sure they have fresh water and protection from the hot sun. Don't store any dog food outside since it will attract insects, rodents, and other dogs. In addition, due to the risk of strangulation — never leave your dog alone while secured to a lead. Likewise, never leave a dog tied up alone in places that have dangerous predators.

This dog has a clean site, plenty of fresh water, and a lot of shade.

Being a Good Neighbor

Keep in mind, many campers and RVers don't even own dogs – let alone travel with them. In fact, some people see dogs as a nuisance. This is another reason why it's important to be a responsible and thoughtful dog owner. Fortunately, at most campgrounds, people tend to take on a "live and let live" attitude about other campers and RVers. As a result, most campers are surprisingly tolerant of dogs (as well as their owners). Nonetheless, there are still a number of unwritten rules about camping and RVing with dogs that you should be aware of. These are some of the most significant ones:

Respect the views of others	Some people are uneasy about large dogs or certain breeds. Consequently, when we're walking our German Shepherd dogs, we move them out of the way to let other people go by. Also, whenever we're staying at a crowded campground – we try to walk them at odd hours. Incidentally, most people walk their dogs between seven and nine in the morning, before and after dinner, and later in the evening (depending on the season and the location).
Never let your dog run loose	Never let your dog roam freely around a campground. If you can't see your dog, you can't control them. It's not only the best way to lose your dog – it'll also result in numerous complaints.

Pick up after your dog

Always pick up after your dog. This helps to keep the area clean, making it more enjoyable for others. It also helps to ensure that dogs will be welcome in the future. If the campground doesn't have conveniently located trash containers – take the bag back to your site and toss it into a small (plastic lined) covered container that is kept outside.

Some campgrounds provide bags to help you pick up after your dog.

Don't let your dog bark continually	No one wants to hear a dog barking incessantly. If your dog barks all the time, find some way to get them under control. If they're outside in a pen, bring them in. If this doesn't work, consider keeping them at home. Remember, for a lot of folks, camping and RVing is the only time they get to relax. If you're not sure whether or not your dog barks when you're gone, install a baby monitor (or a walkie-talkie) and see what happens when you leave.
Don't let your dog lunge at other dogs	Some dogs have an annoying habit of lunging at anything that walks by their campsite. If this is your dog – train them to remain calm under these circumstances. It's not fair to let your dog terrorize people that are simply taking their dog for a walk. One possibility is to use your vehicle to block your dog's view of the road.
Be especially careful around children	The fastest way to generate complaints is to have a dog that scares children. If your dog has a habit of barking or jumping at kids, keep them inside or leave them home. Most campgrounds and RV parks are essentially provisional neighborhoods. Accordingly, families have a right to feel safe and relaxed.

Be careful of other dogs that are loose	When walking your dog, be careful when approaching other dogs that are running free. This situation can often lead to a scuffle or worse. If you're having a problem with a dog that's running around loose – contact the hosts.
Know the rules	As a dog owner, try to get a copy of the campground's pet policy. This will give you two advantages. Firstly, it will help you to comply with the rules. Secondly, you'll be better equipped to fend off frivolous complaints.
Handle complaints sensibly	If someone does complain about your dog, keep your cool and focus on the complaint, not the person doing the complaining. A sincere apology will usually do the trick. If you become defensive or combative, you'll give the campground owner one more reason to restrict dogs.

TENT LIFE
Tent camping with a dog is a lot of fun. However, for some reason, raccoons, skunks, and porcupines like to explore tent sites in the hope of finding food. When you're getting up in the middle of the night for a bathroom break – bring a flashlight, make a little noise, and keep your dog on a tight leash. Otherwise, you could be in for a long night.

If you leave your tent at night with your dog – watch out for these guys.

Leaving Your Dog at the Campground

Despite rules about leaving dogs unattended at a campground, there are times when you have no choice. For example, if it's a warm day and you need to go to the supermarket for some groceries – you can't leave your dog in your car. Consequently, they have to stay back at the campground. Fortunately, most campgrounds and RV parks don't enforce this particular rule – unless your dog barks incessantly while you're away. In any case, you will need to find a way to ensure that your dog is safe and doesn't become a nuisance while you're gone. On that note, here are some tips from experienced campers:

Don't leave them in a tent	Tents can become excessively warm on sunny days. In addition, with a little determination, many dogs can easily escape from a tent.
Keep them inside	When leaving your dog alone, always keep them inside your RV. Never leave them tied up outside when you're not around because the risk of strangulation is greater than you think. Plus, in some parts of the country, coyotes and mountain lions will take advantage of a dog that's tied-up – even in broad daylight!
If they bark, take them with you	Unfortunately, many RVers don't realize that their dogs bark when they're away. If you have a dog that barks constantly when you're gone – don't leave them alone. It's hard on the dog and even harder on other campers. If you have any doubts about your dog's habits (while you're away), use a baby monitor or a walkie-talkie to see if they bark a lot when you're not there.

Parker (hiding behind the windshield) enjoys barking at anyone who walks by his RV.

In warm weather, have a backup plan	In warm weather, many people often leave their dogs in their RV with the air conditioner running. While this is a good way to make sure your dog stays comfortable, there could be a problem if the air conditioner stops running for any reason. While you should always keep a few windows open and leave your dogs lots of water, it may not be enough to keep them safe on a really warm day. If you have two air conditioners – use both of them if you have enough power. If not, you might risk losing all your air conditioning if you trip a breaker or blow a fuse. In any case, if you have a friend or an obliging neighbor at the campground – leave a key and your cell number. For additional information on this important topic, please refer to the next section *("Automated Monitoring Systems")*.
Block their view	Most dogs like to bark at other dogs that are walking by the campsite. Therefore, to minimize barking, restrict your dog's view of the outside world by closing the curtains or shades. In addition, use your RV's air conditioner or roof fan to block the noise of other dogs walking by.
Leave the TV on	If your dog seems to become anxious when you're away – try leaving the television or radio on. "The Dog

	Whisperer" and "Canine Cops" are very popular these days.
Consider medication	Some dogs bark because they're nervous when they're alone. To reduce anxiety, some dog owners have had success with amitriptyline, dog appeasing pheromones, St. John's Wort, or homeopathic pet medicines. If your dog becomes anxious when you're not there – you might want to look into some of these options.
Consider getting a second dog	If drugs, distractions, and window blocking techniques don't seem to work – consider getting a second dog. Life is always easier when you're not alone. On the other hand, you might simply be doubling your troubles.

Temperature Monitoring Systems

Many campers and RVers often go camping when the weather is warm. As a result, the issue of keeping your dog comfortable when you're away from the campground should be one of your top concerns. In this scenario, most campers leave the air conditioning on. Some people also crack a few windows and give their dogs extra water. However, if your RV is in the sun or it's a particularly warm day – your dog will be in big trouble if your air conditioning stops running for any reason.

While contemporary RV air conditioners are fairly reliable, there are a number of things that can go wrong including a power outage at the campground, a bad capacitor, a defective thermostat, an iced-up condenser, or simply a blown fuse. If any of these problems were to occur while you were out, it would only be a matter of time before your RV turned into a sweltering oven.

This is when automated temperature monitoring systems make sense. Designed to alert you when the internal temperature of your RV reaches a certain level – these systems can be a real life saver for people with pets. Here are a few products that could work well in an RV:

Table 2 – Automated Temperature Monitoring Systems

Monitoring System	Description
Temperature Guard SM-VM-500-3	Requires either a land line or a cell phone. Sends out an automated message if temperature exceeds a pre-set limit. Also notifies user if power is out for greater than five minutes. It uses built-in batteries and thus requires no external power supply. **www.safehomeproducts.com**
F Series K-9 Deployment And Heat Alert Systems	Designed for police vehicles (K-9 units) but suitable for an RV, these dash mounted units send out an automated message to a pager if internal temperature exceeds a pre-set limit. The control unit connects to your vehicle's batteries and the pager uses rechargeable batteries. **www.rayallen.com**
Omegaphone Model OMA-VM500-3	Sends out an automated message to a land line phone or pager if temperature exceeds a pre-set limit. Operates on 120 VAC or battery back-up. Note: Requires a land line based phone

	(cannot be used with a cell phone). **www.omega.com**
Temperature@lert Standard 3.5	Monitors the ambient temperature and alerts you via e-mail when it rises or falls outside a preset range. Temperature@lert connects to your PC via an available USB port. Powered by your computer's USB port and never needs new batteries or an AC power adapter. The customizable alert message can be sent continuously or just once when an alert is triggered. Requires access to PC or handheld PDA. **www.temperaturealert.com**
Mobile Temperature Alarm and Phone Dialer	Requires two cell phones. If temperature exceeds a pre-set limit, one cell phone (attached to the unit) calls the other cell phone. It keeps calling every 10 minutes until the # key is pressed. You can call at any time to check your RV's temperature. **www.tiptemp.com**
The Pet Safety Heat Alarm	12 volt system has a 12' extension cord which plugs into your cigarette lighter/DC outlet. If temperature exceeds a pre-set limit, unit will call you. Works with cell phone or two-way radios. **http://sunnyparkrv.com**

Other Backup Solutions

The automated temperature monitoring systems described above are specifically designed to notify you if the internal temperature of your RV exceeds a pre-set level. However, here are some other backup solutions that can be used to help keep your dog safe when unexpected problems crop up:

Thermostatic Controlled Roof Fans

In the event that your RV's air conditioning system fails for any reason, the interior will quickly heat up to the point where it may become intolerable for a dog. In this scenario, the ability to quickly bring fresh air into your RV could be the difference between life and death. This is why thermostatically controlled roof fans are an ideal solution for RVers with dogs.

These cutting-edge products essentially use an integrated thermostat to control the roof fan's on and off switch. When the internal temperature of your RV reaches a pre-set level, the fan automatically turns on (or off). These units are relatively easy to install and will fit in the same 14" x 14" opening that is used for all RV roof fans and vents.

Some models offer a remote control so you don't have to leave the sofa. Other models have covers that shut automatically if it begins to rain. The three leading manufacturers of thermostatically controlled roof fans are Fan-tastic Vent Corporation (**http://www.fantasticvent.com**), MaxxAir Vent Corporation (**www.maxxair.com**), and SHURflo (**www.shurflo.com**).

PROVIDE A SOURCE OF FRESH AIR
Thermostatically controlled roof fans are designed to operate when the temperature inside your RV reaches a certain level. However, these fans will not be able to cool your RV down quickly unless you provide an adequate source of fresh air. The solution – leave a few windows partially open at all times.

One major advantage of thermostatically controlled roof fans is the fact that they operate off the RV's 12-volt electrical system. This means that they'll still work even if there is a power outage at the campground or your AC generator shuts off (assuming it's on in the first place).

Auto-Start Generator Products

If you leave your air conditioner running in your RV to keep your dog comfortable while you're away, there could be a serious problem if there's a power failure. Fortunately, there is a back-up solution that is designed specifically to address this scenario. Known as auto-start generator systems, these units are basically designed to start an RV's generator under certain pre-specified conditions.

One of the most common is the Cumins Onan EC-30 control system. This control is linked to an RV's thermostat so if the interior temperature of the RV goes above a pre-set level, the thermostat sends a signal to the EC-30 telling it to auto-start the generator. According to their website, the EC-30 will first check for shore power. If none is present, the EC-30 will direct the generator to run as long as necessary to maintain the pre-set temperature level.

Many of the newer RVs have the Cummins Onan EC-30 control installed at the factory. For those that do not come equipped with the EC-30 or a similar auto-start system, a new option is the wireless EC-30W. This control functions similarly to the EC-30 except it has its own built-in thermostat, so there's no need to link it to the air conditioner thermostat. For more information, go to **www.cumminsonan.com/rv**.

Friends and Family

A couple of summers ago, when we were staying in a campground in Arizona, we met a woman that was RVing with a female lab and four puppies. Being a dog lover, we kept a vigilant eye on her RV whenever she was away. One day, she didn't come back to her RV. The next day was especially hot but there was still no sign of the woman.

Finally that evening, we called the local sheriff and told him about the dog and the puppies in the RV. He came out to the site and had to break into the RV to get the dogs out. Animal control was called in and the dogs were taken to a safe place. It turned out that the owner was in an accident and ended up in the hospital. Unfortunately – no one knew about the dogs in the RV except us.

When it comes to the safety of your dog, it's hard to put all your faith in technology. After all, the reason we're looking at all these back-up solutions in the first place is because we don't really trust the technology we already have. Besides, as the story about the woman and the puppies illustrates – not every problem can be solved with technology.

When we stay at a campground for an extended period of time, we often make a deal with some of the other campers. We agree to keep an eye on their RVs and they agree to keep an eye on ours. If there's a power failure, we make sure their pets have plenty of fresh air. If their plumbing springs a leak, we shut of the water. You get the idea. It's simple, cheap, and as reliable as any high-tech solution available today.

If you don't plan to spend much time at a specific campground, talk to the manager and see if someone can give you a call if the power goes out. Even if you don't utilize this arrangement as a primary back-up solution, it's a terrific way to get some piece of mind. After all – it's the same system we've been using for nearly 200,000 years.

Activities for Your Dogs

Playing with your dog can provide exercise, enforce training goals, reduce stress, and lower the incidence of problematic behaviors (such as barking). While the number of possible pet-related activities is virtually unlimited, the following list should get you started:

Swimming	If your dog enjoys the water (many do), let them go in for a dip. If you're on a lake with a dock, let them dive into the water. If you're staying near the ocean, let them frolic in the tidal zone. Bring plenty of towels and watch out for fishing lines, power boats, jet skis, and broken glass along the shoreline.

Most dogs love swimming and playing in the water.

Picnics	Our dog's favorite hobby is begging. What better activity for the begging dog than a picnic. Be sure to bring some extra food. That way – you'll be able to have something to eat too.
Ball or Frisbee toss	Even if your dog isn't a champion athlete, they'll still enjoy chasing after a Frisbee or a tennis ball. It's terrific exercise and maybe you can even teach your dog to give it back once in a while.
Campfires	There's something timeless about sitting around a campfire under the stars with your dog. You can commemorate the occasion by roasting up a few wieners. Needless to say, treasured moments like this tend to go better with beer.

CAMPFIRE CAUTION

Each year, numerous dogs get seriously burned by campfires. Some are injured when a spark or an ember lands on them. Others are hurt when they lay too close to the fire and the logs unexpectedly shift. As a result, don't let your dog get too close to the fire and always keep a pail of water nearby, just in case. To treat burns, please refer to Chapter 9.

Walks, jogging, and hiking	Dogs are always a great excuse to go on a hike; Bring plenty of water, take some treats, stay on the trails, and keep them on their leash.

For some dog owners, winter camping offers a number of unique recreational opportunities.

Agility training	We've seen people set up chairs, hoops, tables, and camping gear to create a makeshift obstacle course for their dog. It's a blast to watch as their dogs soar over the stuff (or not).
Boating	If your dog likes the water, they'll probably enjoy boating. If you plan

121

on fishing though, be careful because most dogs like to help. Always put a life preserver on you as well as your dog.

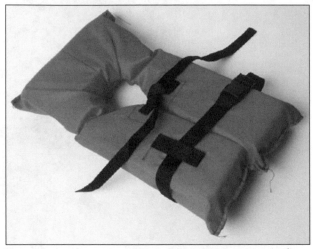

If you take your dog out in a boat, put a life preserver on your dog (as well as yourself).

Playing with other dogs	Sometimes it seems that dogs are their happiest when they're frolicking with other dogs. If you're lucky – you'll meet some campers with friendly dogs that like to play.
Photo sessions	Go on a nature hike and snap away while your dog enjoys his walk. Be sure to include your dog in some of the photos. For additional information, please see next page.

Ten Tips for Taking Great Dog Photos

It's not always easy to take a good picture of a dog. However, the following techniques are frequently used by professional pet photographers to get really great shots. Grab your dog, get your camera, and click away.

When it comes to taking a photo of a dog – you can never be too close.

1. Familiarize your dog to the camera – In order to get natural photos of your dog, he must be comfortable with the equipment. Let your dog have a close look at your camera. Turn it on and click the shutter several times until he's familiar with the sound. Also, hold the camera while letting your dog smell and sniff the camera (don't let him lick it!). Once your dog is familiar with your camera – you'll be able to take all the pictures you want.

2. Take a ton of pictures – Assuming you're using a digital camera, take a lot of photos. In fact, according to most professional photographers – they get one or two great shots out of every one hundred shots they take. There are two caveats to remember though when taking a lot of digital photos: 1) make sure your battery is charged fully and 2) make sure you have enough memory to store lots of photos.

3. Bend over or sit down – Just as with babies, a portrait photo always comes out better if you take it approximately at eye level. That way, the photo won't seem like you're looking down on your subject.

4. Frame the background of the photo – Try to find an appealing and uncluttered background for your dog portrait. Simple is better. Also, make sure there are no trees or branches in the background. Otherwise, it might look like they're growing out of your dog's head. You can, however, use the arch of a tree branch or a rock wall or

other natural features to "frame" your dog. Also, you can use the portrait setting (or a large aperture setting) to blur the background and put all of the focus and emphasis on your dog's face.

5. Look for the sun – Find the sun and put it to your back. This puts the sun on your dog's face and allows people to see more of your dog's features. You can also take some nice photos with the sun on either side of your dog as well.

6. Don't use a flash inside – If you can find another source of light indoors, you should use that instead of a flash. A flash can cause red-eye or green-eye in dogs. If you have a removable flash or one that you can aim away from your dog, that will work beautifully.

7. Leave some room – If you're taking an action shot or a photo of your dog doing something, leave some room around the dog. People like to look at photos in which it looks like the dog has room to move forward (as opposed to being cramped and cut-off).

8. Get as close as possible – A great photo portrait is a close one. You don't even have to get your dog's entire face in the photo. Of course, getting real close to your dog can sometimes be a problem because he may try to sniff the camera. Here's where a telephoto lens can come in handy. You can be a little bit away from your dog and still get a great close-up by zooming in on his face.

9. Use a color appropriate background – If your dog is all black, obviously you should consider using a light background for your dog's photos. Also, try to find a natural environment that complements your dog's coloring. For example, our red and tan German Shepherd dog looks terrific in the fall with leaves all around.

10. Experiment and have fun – Don't be afraid to try something new. Some of the best photos we've taken are purely experimental and silly. Also, play with your dog inside or out while someone snaps photos. You'll be guaranteed to get some good ones.

What to Do if your Dog Gets Lost

Losing a dog during a camping trip is more common than you think. However, if you do lose track of your dog, there are a number of things you can do that will significantly increase your odds of finding your dog. On that note – here are some tips from the experts:

| **Make your dog easy to find** | Chapter 4 includes a section titled "The Best Ways to Keep Track of your Dog". This section describes some of the products and technologies that are used today to identify as well as locate lost dogs. |

Look around and call their name	When you first lose sight of your dog, don't run off to find your dog. Instead, stay in the area and call their name loud and clear. If your voice doesn't carry, create a makeshift megaphone from a rolled-up piece of cardboard or newspaper. Don't give up until you can't shout anymore.
Talk to other campers	Walk around and talk to other campers. Show them a picture (or a drawing) of your dog and be sure to leave your phone number.
Leave something behind	If you have to leave the area (without finding your dog), attach a piece of your clothing to a tree. If your dog returns while you're away – they'll usually stay by the object assuming that you'll be back to retrieve it.
Use the press	Place a "Lost Pet" ad in the local newspaper. Be sure to check the "Found" section each day.
Post fliers	Take a photo of your dog to any office supply store (i.e. Kinko's). They'll help you to create a lost pet poster. Be sure to offer a reward since it'll improve the odds of getting your dog back. Start by placing the poster in the area where your dog was last seen. Then expand out from there.

| Don't get swindled | Unfortunately, there are con artists that will use lost pet posters to rip people off. As a result, never agree to meet someone alone; never give out your address; and don't give out any reward money until you actually have your dog back. |

Workcamping with a Dog

Many of the people that work at RV parks and campgrounds are work campers. Work campers are essentially volunteers that agree to work at a campground in exchange for a free site and other benefits. Some also receive an hourly wage. Work camping is very popular with seasonal and full-time RVers that enjoy staying involved with campground operations and other activities. Some serve as guides at popular tourist attractions while others perform maintenance or register guests.

Work campers typically find employment opportunities by contacting parks and campgrounds they're interested in and by looking through work camping openings listed in "Workamper News". For further information, visit **www.workamper.com**. Fortunately, having a dog doesn't affect your ability to become a work camper. In fact, many work campers have dogs and most enjoy taking them with them as they perform their duties. Some even direct dog hikes where dozens of campers (and their dogs) get together to explore the local trails.

Handling Unique Environments

Camping with a dog will enable you to explore
lots of exciting new places.

Campers and RVers are unquestionably some of the most
mobile people in the world. In fact, many full-time RVers
spend their entire life traveling from place to place. While
mobility is clearly one of the things that makes camping and
RVing so appealing – it also means that you'll inevitably find
yourself in places that are very different from what you're
used to. Accordingly, this chapter is designed to help you deal
with some of the nation's most challenging environments.

The Desert

The desert represents one of the toughest natural
environments in the world due to a severe lack of water,

intense heat, treacherous plant life, and deadly predators. It's also one of the most beautiful places on earth.

In spite of its intimidating nature, the Sonoran desert is a popular destination for campers and RVers who travel with dogs.

Here are some things to keep in mind when camping in the desert with your dog:

Bring lots of water

Last September, a couple with two dogs was returning from a modest hike in the Arizona desert. One of the dogs was having difficulty walking so the owner carried the dog the rest of the way. Within fifteen minutes – both dogs were dead from heatstroke and dehydration. Apparently, they hadn't brought enough water for all four of them.

When hiking in the desert with your dog, bring plenty of water and a container for drinking. Camping stores sell specialized backpacks that are designed to hold and dispense water. They also sell collapsible bowls that can be folded up and stuffed in your pocket. If your dog starts panting or seems out of breath, slowly give them some water and take a break until their breathing is normal. Then immediately head back to your campsite.

Be aware of Valley Fever	If you're staying in the southwestern United States, you should be aware of a potentially debilitating disease known as Valley Fever. Since the disease is caused by a fungus in the soil, dogs often become infected as a result of digging in dry, dusty areas. Call a local vet to see if the area you're in has a high incidence of Valley Fever. If it does, ask your vet for suggestions.
Clean up after your dog	If you're walking your dog on a path in the desert, pick up and properly dispose of your dog's waste.
Use current ID tags	Once again, make sure that your dog's collar has an ID tag that includes their name and your phone number. Better yet, use a GPS enabled collar. For additional information, please refer to Chapter 4.

IN THE DESERT, KEEP THEM ON A LEASH
In the desert, when a dog runs free, they invariably get covered in prickly clumps of cactus. Eventually, they can hardly move. Coyotes know how to remove the clumps of cactus but domesticated dogs don't have a clue. When you're in the desert with your dog, keep them on a leash and watch the ground.

The desert is full of strange plants that can be hazardous to both humans and dogs.

Coping with Dangerous Desert Plants

Water is a precious commodity in the desert. Consequently, most of the plants that grow in the desert preserve the little water they have by keeping predators away. Accordingly, desert plants can be a real challenge to campers and their dogs.

Here are some of the tricks used by experienced desert campers with dogs:

| **Get an illustrated field guide** | If you plan on staying in the desert for a while, try to become familiar with the plants and animals that live there. Knowledge is always the best tool for ensuring your safety. |

Test the ground for thorns	If your dog is new to the desert, gently press the palm of your hand on the ground in a few different locations. If small thorns, needles, or prickly seeds stick to your hand, don't proceed. Otherwise, your dog's paws will quickly become imbedded with these same thorns and needles. Luckily, your dog will eventually develop thickened pads to protect them from most thorns.
Bring a comb and a pair of pliers	When taking your dog for a walk in the desert, always bring a comb and a pair of pliers. The comb is highly effective at flicking away pieces of cactus that will inevitably latch onto your dog. The pliers are used for pulling out individual thorns that can't be combed out. Never, ever remove pieces of cactus or thorns with your fingers. If you try – you'll end up in the same prickly predicament as your dog.
Remove stray pieces of Cholla	Once you get settled in, conduct a visual survey of your campsite to identify and remove any stray pieces of cactus in the immediate area. Use barbeque tongs, a rake, a stick, or even pliers to move them out of the way. Don't use your hands or your feet.
Watch out for wind and rain	After a wind storm, avoid walking your dog anywhere near Cholla cactus. The

	wind will have dislodged dozens of prickly pieces of Cholla that will lay in wait like Velcro™ land mines.
Train your dog to avoid cactus	You can actually teach your dog to stay away from dangerous plants. Whenever they approach certain plants, quickly pull on their leash while using a consistent and highly recognizable command. After a while, they'll figure it out.
Watch out for any swelling	Some cactus thorns are capable of producing severe physical reactions. If you see any swelling in your dog's paws, take them to a vet right away. Antibiotics and anti-inflammatory drugs will usually clear things up in a few days. For minor irritations, apply a little hydrocortisone ointment.
Consider using booties	If you're going to be hiking in the desert with your dog, consider fitting them with booties. Pet stores sell leather or vinyl versions that are highly effective at protecting a dog's paws. However, be careful when you remove the booties since they may be imbedded with cactus thorns.
Observe your dog's behavior	Closely watch your dog's behavior when walking in the desert. If they begin to limp, favor one leg, or start lifting a paw, stop immediately and examine their

paws for thorns. Be sure to run your fingers between their toes. If you find a piece of cactus, remove it without delay. Eventually, your dog will lift their paw to tell you they've stepped on something sharp. After you remove the piece of cactus, reward them for telling you about it. At the end of each day, use a flashlight to check for small burrs, barbs, and thorns that you might have missed.

Avoiding Predators in the Desert

The creatures that live in the desert represent some of the toughest and shrewdest survivors anywhere on the planet. By comparison – family dogs are like pampered rich kids from the suburbs. Consequently, pay close attention to this section.

Keep an eye on the brush	Don't walk your dog through shrubs or thick brush during the warmer months. These locations will often harbor venomous snakes and scorpions.
Never leave them alone	 Do not leave your dog tied up alone in the desert. Mountain lions have been known to kill dogs while they were on a leash. Mountain lions are shrewd predators that will exploit any opportunity to obtain a meal.

Keep your dog on a leash	Never, ever let your dog roam freely in the desert. Between cactus, snakes, scorpions, and coyotes – there's a lot that can happen.
Keep them away from holes	Practically everything in the desert lives or sleeps under the ground. As a result, the desert is full of holes. Don't let your dog dig in any of them. They might be surprised at what crawls out.
Watch out for coyotes	Coyotes are generally timid creatures but they are very formidable when in a pack. Therefore, never let a group of coyotes surround you (or your dog). If you do encounter a pack of coyotes – take a firm hold of your dog's leash and leave the area. Never, ever let your dog off its leash around coyotes. If you do – you may never see your dog again. Really.

Remember, coyotes know more about your dog than you do.

BUT DO THEY HOWL AT THE MOON...
In the Sonoran Desert, domesticated dogs get lost all the time. Most last less than 24 hours but a few of them adapt in ways you wouldn't believe. Recently, a local ranger saw a small pack of coyotes chasing down a desert hare. Included in the pack were a beagle and a pit bull mix.

Use a flashlight	When walking your dog at night, always use a strong flashlight to see where you're going. The flashlight will also enable vehicles, other campers, and wildlife to see you coming.
Be careful of the dark	The majority of desert predators are partially nocturnal. In fact, snakes, scorpions, coyotes, and javelinas do much of their hunting on warm summer nights. During that time, we always keep our dogs on the campground roads.
Learn how to deal with snake bites	If your dog does get bitten by a snake, keep them calm and take them quickly to a local animal emergency care facility. See Chapter 9 for details.
Make some noise	It's best not to surprise a predator (especially at night). Consequently, when you're walking in the desert, make some noise as you proceed. By talking, whistling, or singing, you'll give the creatures that live there a little time to move on.

Stay away from javelinas	Although they tend to avoid people, javelinas are fairly common in desert environments. They look like hairy pigs, but that's where the similarity ends. If threatened (especially if there are babies around), javelinas may begin an offensive stampede. They've been clocked at 25 mph and can literally soar through the air up to 9 feet! In a number of instances, dogs have been seriously injured and even killed. If you see any javelinas – keep your dog quiet and immediately leave the area.

Forest Lands

Most dogs love the woods. There's always an infinite variety of smells and an abundance of interesting wildlife. However, like all natural environments, forests pose their own unique set of challenges.

Use pet IDs or a GPS collar	At the risk of sounding like a broken record, be sure that your dog has a current ID tag. If they get lost in the woods, the tag will become a crucial source of hope. A GPS enabled collar is your best bet. Please see Chapter 4 for details.
Be careful taking your dog off its leash	The decision to let your dog off its leash should be made cautiously. For instance, if there are deer in the area –

keep your dog on a leash. Dogs often get lost when they chase deer because they ignore where (and how far) they've gone. Similarly, if trapping is legal, don't let them run free for obvious reasons.

Even a trained dog will often chase a deer.

Stay off posted land	If the land you're hiking on is posted with "No Trespassing" signs, take another route. In some parts of the country, people will shoot dogs that trespass on their property. No kidding.
Watch out for bees	Bee keeping is a popular activity in many rural areas. If you encounter a collection of stacked boxes or crates in a sunny location, steer clear. It could be somebody's prized bee collection.

Similarly, your dog may unintentionally stumble upon an active bee hive. Today, many hives contain Africanized bees that are extremely aggressive, especially when threatened. Africanized bees have been known to kill dogs as well as people.

Don't let your dog drink the water

Giardia is a microscopic parasite that lives in intestines of many domestic and wild animals. As a result, it is frequently found in ponds and streams. Unfortunately, Giardia can be transmitted to both humans and dogs. Signs of infection are diarrhea, depression, weight loss, decreased appetite, and vomiting. If left untreated, it erodes the intestinal lining and will cause bloody diarrhea as well as leave the animal susceptible to other infections. Fortunately, there is a vaccine available. While it's not completely foolproof, it does offer some protection.

Avoid dangerous plants

Don't let your dog eat mushrooms or other woodland plants (except grass) because they may be poisonous. There are illustrated guide books that can help you to identify dangerous plants. If your dog gets into something like poison ivy – bathe them immediately using a gentle shampoo and warm water. Be sure to wear rubber gloves and keep the soap and water away from your dog's eyes (to reduce the possibility of spreading the plant's caustic oils). Then take a hot shower to get any oils off your skin.

Poison ivy can be found in most wooded areas.

Be aware of unsafe terrain	Ask around or use a topographic map to determine if there are any dangerous cliffs or steep terrain in the region. If so, stay clear of those areas.

POISONOUS PLANTS TO AVOID

When camping and RVing with a dog, consider bringing an illustrated guide book to help you to identify dangerous or poisonous plants. The following list should get you started:

BULBS: Amaryllis, Autumn Crocus, Daffodil, Day Lily, Elephant Ears, Gladiolas, Hyacinth, Iris, Lily of the Valley, Narcissus, Orange Day Lily, Tulip

FERNS: Asparagus Fern, Australian Nut, Emerald Feather (aka Emerald Fern), Emerald Fern (aka Emerald Feather), Lace Fern, Plumosa Fern

FLOWERING PLANTS: Cyclamen, Hydrangea, Kalanchoe, Poinsettia

GARDEN PERENNIALS: Charming Diffenbachia, Christmas Rose, Flamingo Plant, Foxglove, Marijuana, Morning Glory, Nightshade

LILLIES: Asian Lily (liliaceae), Easter Lily, Glory Lily, Japanese Show Lily, Red Lily, Rubrum Lily, Stargazer Lily, Tiger Lily, Wood Lily

SHRUBS: Cycads, Heavenly Bamboo, Holly, Jerusalem Cherry, Mistletoe "American", Oleander, Precatory Bean, Rhododendron, Saddle Leaf Philodendron, Sago Palm, Tree Philodendron, Yucca

TREES: Avocado, Buddhist Pine, Chinaberry Tree, Japanese Yew (aka Yew), Lacy Tree, Macadamia Nut, Madagascar Dragon Tree, Queensland Nut, Schefflera, Yew (aka Japanese Yew)

> **VINES:** Branching Ivy, English Ivy, European Bittersweet, Glacier Ivy, Hahn's self branching English Ivy, Needlepoint Ivy
>
> **MISCELLANEOUS:** American Bittersweet, Andromeda Japonica, Azalea, Bird of Paradise, Buckeye, Caladium hortulanum, Calla Lily, Castor Bean, Clematis, Fiddle-Leaf Philodendron, Florida Beauty, Fruit Salad Plant, Golden Dieffenbachia, Gold Dust Dracaena, Heartleaf Philodendron, Horsehead Philodendron, Hurricane Plant, Mexican Breadfruit, Mother-in-law, Panda, Philodendron Pertusum, Red Emerald, Red Princess, Ribbon Plant, Satin Pothos, Spotted Dumb Cane, Sweetheart Ivy, Swiss Cheese Plant, variable Dieffenbachia, Variegated Philodendron, Yesterday/Today/Tomorrow

Dealing with Insects

Most wooded environments have an abundant supply of biting and stinging insects. Here are a few pointers from experienced deep-woods campers:

Use heartworm medication	Heartworm is a deadly disease (in dogs) that's transmitted by mosquitoes. If you're in an area with an active mosquito population – make sure that your dog is taking heartworm medication. Dogs should be tested annually for heartworm disease before taking the medication. If they have the disease, they'll need to be treated right away.

Apply insect repellent	If you're camping in the woods, be sure to use bug repellent on your dog. Their ears, eyes, mouth, and stomach are the most vulnerable. Cover their eyes and follow the directions on the label. In general, the greater the percentage of deet – the more effective the repellent. Use as little as possible to prevent your dog from licking or ingesting the bug repellent.
Bring hydrocortisone	Hydrocortisone ointment is highly effective at reducing the itching and burning that occurs when a dog is bitten or stung by an insect. It's also effective for people. Keep a tube handy.
Watch out for insect nests	Keep an eye out for wasp and hornet nests. These cone-shaped paper nests are often attached to tree limbs, but they sometimes fall to the ground. Yellow jackets, in contrast, often reside in ground nests that can't be detected until it's too late.
Use flea and tick medication	If you're staying in a wooded area during the spring and summer months, make sure that your dog is being treated with a topical flea and tick medication such as Frontline™. Avoid camping in areas that are notoriously infested with ticks (i.e. Cape Cod, Massachusetts). Deer ticks are the primary carriers of Lyme disease, a

	serious illness that can affect both dogs and people. Examine your dog (and yourself) for ticks every day.
Remove ticks immediately	For Lyme disease to spread, a tick must be attached for at least 48 hours. Therefore, if you find a tick on your dog (or on you), remove it right away. First try using an alcohol soaked swab. If this doesn't work, use tweezers to take hold of the tick where its mouth is attached to your dog's skin. Don't use a match or a cigarette to extract the tick. If the tick's head stays under the dog's skin – leave it. It will eventually fall out.

Dealing with Animals in Wooded Areas

The majority of animals that pose a threat to dogs are nocturnal. If you keep your dog out of the woods from dusk to dawn, they'll probably be safe from most animals (except bears and mountain lions). Here are a few more tips for keeping them safe and sound:

Stay clear of skunks	Skunks aren't usually active until dusk. If your dog does get sprayed, bathe them immediately. Some people use fruit juice or tomato juice but soap and water seems to work just as well. You can also use special pet products that are

supposed to be effective at eliminating skunk odors. In the real world – expect to live with the smell for at least several weeks.

GOOD THING HE HAD A DOG...
A friend of ours with a large dog was camping in the Maine woods a few years ago. One night, they both woke up to a loud sniffing and snorting sound. His dog, frozen from fear, sat in the center of the tent. When the sound stopped, he peered outside to see who was stopping by for a late night sniff. When he unzipped the door to the tent – a small black bear slipped away into the darkness.

Be careful of porcupines	Like skunks, porcupines are primarily nocturnal. If your dog gets skewered by a porcupine, try to get them to a vet as quickly as possible. If this isn't an option, use wire cutters or scissors to trim off all but an inch of each quill. Then use pliers to quickly pull out the quills, one at a time. Examine the inside of your dog's mouth to make sure that you haven't missed any. Then get them to a vet ASAP.
Protect your dog from rabies	Since many wild animals are rabid – make sure that your dog is up-to-date on their rabies shots.
Don't go camping with bears	Bears are extremely formidable predators. If you're camping in a section of the country that has bears – never

walk in thick underbrush. Instead, stay in open areas where the visibility is good. Stay far away from bears that have cubs around. Never let your dog off its leash if you're in bear country. Bring a pepper spray device that's designed specifically for bears. Marine air horns are also used as a deterrent by some campers. The bottom line: Stay away from bears.

WATCH OUT FOR ALLIGATORS

Florida and Louisiana have over a million alligators each. As a result, several dogs are killed by these prehistoric creatures each year. If you're camping or RVing in alligator country – keep your dog away from any body of water that is capable of supporting alligators. As a practical matter, this includes almost any wetland, pond, stream, river, tributary, or lake.

Alligators are a genuine threat to dogs and people in some areas.

Freshwater and Marine Environments

Whether it's the ocean, a lake, or even a puddle, dogs like to splash around and get wet. If you're staying at a park or a campground near a body of water, there are a few things that you should keep in mind:

Clean up after your dog	While on the beach, clean up after your dog. Don't simply bury it in the sand or fling it in the water.
Teach your dog to enjoy the water	Most dogs take to the water naturally. However, if you have a puppy or a young dog; give them time to get accustomed to the water. Play with them on the shore or on the beach but don't force them to go in the water. If you take it slow and let them experiment at their own pace – they'll inevitably discover the delightful world of getting wet.

This dog understands that fishing takes perseverance.

Comply with local ordinances	Most beach environments are regulated, so make sure that you're complying with any ordinances relating to dogs. They usually involve keeping your dog on a leash or staying off certain beaches.
Don't assume the water's safe	If you're camping by a lake that's located within a populated area, the water could be polluted. If your dog does goes in – give them a bath and clean their ears (afterwards) with a pet product that's designed for preventing ear infections.
Avoid fishing areas	Stay out of areas where people are fishing. In marine environments, make sure that your dog avoids buoy lines, fish nets, fish hooks, lures, and other sub-surface hazards.
Be careful of power boats	If your dog likes to go in the water, look out for power boats, water skiers, or jet skis.
Watch out for hidden currents	Calm looking ocean waves can often conceal dangerous currents and rip tides. If you see warning signs about dangerous tides, stay out of the water. If you do get carried out to sea by a rip tide – don't try to swim back to shore. Instead, swim to your left or right (parallel to the shore) until you can swim back towards the shore. The idea is to first get out of the rip tide's region of influence before

attempting to swim back. Life preservers are also a good idea for both of you.

Hidden currents and sub-surface rip tides are responsible for many deaths every year.

Avoid certain beaches	Some beaches have razor-sharp mussel shells and barnacle-covered rocks that can tear up your dog's paws. Before your dog hits the beach, check it out.
Bathe your dog if they've been in the ocean	If your dog has been swimming in the ocean, bathe them when they get out. Salt water can leave your dog's coat feeling greasy for days. In the meantime – they'll smell like an old plate of fried clams.
Learn what's in the water	Keep your dog out of ponds that have snapping turtles or water moccasins (a venomous freshwater snake). These

creatures can injure or actually kill a dog. Similarly, some coastal beaches in southern waters have stinging jellyfish. Check with the locals before you let your dog in for a swim.

Don't let them chase wildlife	Don't allow your dog to swim after ducks or geese because they might encounter a beaver. Beavers, unfortunately, have the skills to drown a swimming dog.

Camping Near Cities

Cities are considered to be one of the more challenging environments for campers and RVers with dogs. However, if you check out any major urban area – you'll witness an endless variety of well-adjusted city dogs.

If your dog is well trained, there's no reason to keep them away from the city.

Most dog owners stay in campgrounds outside the city and simply take their dog with them when they go in. The following suggestions are based on extensive experience with dogs in the city:

Keep a tight rein on your dog	Never let your dog off its leash unless you're in a designated dog play area. If your dog gets lost in the city – you're in for a long, stressful ordeal.
Make sure your dog is vaccinated	Rabies vaccinations are mandatory in the city. Consequently, make sure that your dog has a tag indicating the date of their last rabies vaccination.
Take advantage of city parks	If your dog isn't accustomed to urban settings, it can be difficult to get them to do their "business" on paved surfaces. Fortunately, most cities have numerous small parks and promenades where they can enjoy the numerous benefits of real grass.
Always keep your dog on a leash	Most cities have strictly enforced leash laws. If you want to avoid getting a ticket  from the local animal control authorities – keep your dog on a leash.

Keep your dog on a short leash and close by your side.

Comply with dog curbing laws	Most cities impose sizable fines on dog owners that don't "curb" their dog. Curbing is an outdated term that now means cleaning up after your dog. Curbing used to mean training your dog to go to the bathroom in the street (beyond the curb).

Urban Hazards in the City

The following recommendations are intended to minimize some of the risks that dogs in the city face:

Avoid empty city lots	Abandoned city lots (known as "brownfields") typically contain hidden toxic chemicals, hazardous materials, contaminated soil, and various physical hazards. Keep your dog away from them.
Keep them away from puddles	Never let your dog drink from a puddle in the city. They often contain antifreeze, motor oil, and gasoline.
Cross the streets like a local	When crossing city streets, keep your dog close to your side. Always obey traffic signals and wait until there's a crowd before you cross (there's safety in numbers). When crossing the street – never let your dog take the lead and don't ever run.

Teach your dog to drop things	Cities tend to have a lot of debris and garbage. As a result, make sure that you've trained your dog to drop objects that they've picked up.
Watch out for hot asphalt	If you're walking your dog in the summer, watch out for hot streets and sidewalks. Some paved surfaces get so hot; they'll blister your dog's paws.
Protect your dog from theft	If you must leave your dog in a parked vehicle, lock the car and leave the windows open a little (assuming it's not too warm). If your dog is aggressive, make sure that a child can't slip their fingers through a partially opened window. If your dog is a sought-after breed – avoid parking in public areas. Instead, park in a garage or a private lot.

Dealing with People in the City

Here are a few other things to keep in mind when you take your dog into the city:

Consider using a muzzle	If your dog has aggressive tendencies, put a muzzle on them while walking in the city. It might look a little intimidating – but it beats going to court.

Respect your dog's basic nature	Some dogs shouldn't be taken into the city. This includes dogs that are highly protective; naturally aggressive dogs; or dogs that are uneasy about strangers.
Don't let people feed your dog	In the city, well-meaning people will sometimes try to give your dog a treat. Don't allow this to happen. For their own protection – your dog should be trained to never take anything from strangers.

Never let strangers feed your dog.

Don't hesitate to tell people your dog isn't friendly	If your dog is wary of strangers, it's okay to tell people that your dog isn't friendly. Most people will understand and appreciate the heads-up. The ones that don't will eventually recover.

Handling Medical Problems

The principal goal during any camping trip should be
to keep your dog safe and healthy.

While this chapter isn't a substitute for medical training or
genuine veterinarian care, it can help you to decide when it's
time to take your dog in for medical care. It'll also help you to

DO THIS RIGHT NOW
If you really want to increase the odds of saving your dog's
life in a genuine medical emergency – obtain the address
and phone number of the nearest emergency animal
hospital. Purchase a local map and use a marker to show
the exact route to the animal hospital (starting from the
campground). Then put the map in your glove box. If your
dog needs emergency medical care, you'll already know who
to call and where to go. Not bad.

tackle medical emergencies that occur when there's nobody else around.

══ Dealing with Severe Medical ══ Conditions

At some point in time, you may be required to handle a true medical emergency involving your dog that requires you to act immediately. This first section focuses on this possibility.

Take Your Dog to the Vet if you Observe:

If you observe any of the following symptoms, get your dog to a veterinarian right away:

Seizures	Inexplicable Viciousness
Abnormal Lumps	Excessive Water Consumption
Abnormal Posture	Unable to Put Weight on a Limb
Breathing Problems	Discharges from Nose or Eyes
Excessive Vomiting	Persistent Constipation
High Fever (>104° F)	Loss of Hair or Open Sores
Severe Diarrhea	Jaundice
Excessive Drooling	Marked Weight Loss
Loss of Appetite	Excessive Urination
Inability to Urinate	Unable to Stand or Get Up
Sudden Lethargy	Excessive Head Shaking

When a medical emergency occurs, try to remain as calm as possible because in these situations – your dog is entirely dependent on you. If you panic, you may be unable to perform the emergency procedures they so desperately need.

In any serious emergency, there are several things that you should always do.

Make sure your dog is safe and secure	If you're close to traffic, move out of the way. If you're in a burning vehicle, get out. You can't help your dog if you get hurt!
Hang on to your dog	Most dogs try to run away when they get injured. So whatever you do, don't let go of your dog; even if he struggles or tries to bite you.
Get ready to go	Quickly assess your dog's injuries and prepare to take them to an emergency animal care facility. If you suspect internal injuries or broken bones – secure your dog to a flat surface, such as a board or a table. Alternatively, wrap them in a blanket or a coat and secure it with some rope, tape, or a belt.
Do something	 If your dog is choking or unconscious, you won't have time to get to a vet. In this scenario – Your primary goal, in an emergency, should always be to get your dog to a vet as quickly as possible.

159

	almost anything you try is better than nothing. Start by following the directions (in this section) for treating an unconscious or choking dog. When your dog is breathing again, get them to a vet. If there is no vet around, call the numbers on the following page and tell them you have an emergency. Meanwhile, stay as calm as possible.
Use the Internet	If you have a computer with Internet access, perform a search using the keywords: Emergency Vet, City, State (i.e. Emergency Vet, Richmond, Virginia). Also, the following websites assert they can help you to locate a vet in your area: • www.vetquest.com • www.vetlocator.petplace.com • www.healthypet.com
Get a cell phone	In an emergency, you will need to call for help. If you don't have a cell phone; now's the time to get one.
Get help any way you can	Find a vet or an emergency care facility anyway you can. Call 911 if you have to. When you do find a vet, call ahead. This will enable them to assist you over the phone while preparing for your arrival. Be sure to get detailed driving instructions. These two organizations can

provide help in an emergency:

> The American Animal Hospital
> Association
> 1-800-252-2242
>
> The American Veterinary Medical
> Association
> 1-847-925-8070

HOW TO CREATE A MAKESHIFT MUZZLE

In an emergency, you'll probably have to muzzle your dog. Here's how to fashion one from virtually anything.

1. Find a long strip of cloth or a piece of sheeting.

2. Make a noose by tying a knot in the middle of the strip of cloth, effectively creating a large loop.

3. Approach the dog from behind and slip the noose about halfway up their nose. Then pull it tight.

4. Pull the ends back behind the dog's neck and tie them together.

5. If you don't have any cloth, use first aid tape, a belt, or even duct tape. Leave a little space for them to breathe.

Dealing with a Choking Dog

If your dog is choking, you don't have much time. Reach into their mouth and remove any foreign objects. If necessary, pull their tongue out and sweep your fingers around. If you feel something, try to hook it with your fingers and pull it out. If you can't remove the object – perform the Heimlich maneuver.

PERFORMING THE HEIMLICH MANEUVER ON A DOG

If your dog is choking and you are unable to manually remove the obstruction:

1. Lay your dog on their side. Then lie down behind them and put your arms around them.

2. Place one fist in your other hand and give five sharp thrusts (bear hugs) to their abdomen (just below the rib cage).

3. Check to see if there's still something lodged in their airway.

4. If the dog is still choking, use the heel of your hand to give them a sharp thump on the back (between the shoulder blades).

5. If you find something; remove it. If your dog isn't breathing, proceed with artificial respiration (described next).

Performing Artificial Respiration

Artificial respiration is performed when there's no sign of breathing (i.e. your dog's chest isn't moving). If artificial respiration fails to get your dog breathing again, begin

CPR (described in the following section).

Clear their airway	Open your dog's mouth and confirm that their airway is clear. If it isn't, remove any visible obstruction or perform the Heimlich maneuver (as described previously).
Get them Breathing	With large dogs, tilt their head back, firmly close their jaw, and steadily exhale into their nose. For smaller dogs, cover their nose and mouth with your mouth as you exhale. Your dog's chest should expand. Remove your mouth after each breath to allow air to escape. Use the following guide to set the number of breaths per second: **Dogs over 60 lbs:** 1 breath every 5 seconds **Dogs 10 to 60 lbs:** 1 breath every 4 seconds **Dogs under 10 lbs:** 1 breath every 3 seconds

GO EASY ON THE LITTLE GUYS
With small dogs, never exhale forcefully since you might inadvertently injure them. Likewise, when performing chest compressions, press gently to avoid damaging their ribcage.

Performing CPR on Your Dog

CPR is performed when there's no sign of breathing and no heartbeat. If possible, use two people to perform CPR. One can do the breathing while the other does the chest compressions.

BEFORE PERFORMING CPR – REMOVE ANY OBSTRUCTIONS

Before you begin CPR on a dog, make sure there aren't any obstructions in their airway. Obstructions must always be removed *before* doing CPR (even if your dog isn't breathing).

Begin chest compressions	Lay your dog on its side and gently compress the side of its rib cage. Alternatively, you can lay your dog on its back and press on both sides of its rib cage.

Dogs over 60 lbs:
Perform 60 compressions per minute (one compression every second). For large dogs, compress their chest roughly 1 to 2 inches.

Dogs 10 to 60 lbs:
Perform 80 to 100 compressions per minute (three compressions every 2 seconds).

Dogs less than 10 lbs:
Perform 120 compressions per minute (two compressions every second).

Alternate Breaths with Compressions	Start alternating breaths with compressions until your dog begins to breathe on their own. **Small dogs and puppies:** Perform one breath for every two chest compressions. **Medium dogs:** Perform one breath for every four chest compressions. **Large dogs (over 120 lbs.):** Perform one breath for every five chest compressions.

NEVER PRACTICE CPR ON A HEALTHY DOG
Don't perform artificial respiration or chest compressions on a healthy dog. If you do, you could unintentionally hurt or even kill them.

Checking Your Dog's Pulse

The easiest place to locate a pulse is along the femoral artery in your dog's groin area. Place your fingers on the inside of their hind leg and slide your hand upward until the back of your fingers touch their abdomen. Gently move your fingers back and forth on the inside of the hind leg until you feel a pulse. Count the number of pulses in fifteen seconds and multiply that number by four. This will give you the number of beats per minute (bpm). These are the normal resting heart rates for different size dogs:

Small dogs: 90 to 160 bpm

Medium dogs: 70 to 110 bpm

Large dogs: 60 to 90 bpm

Checking Your Dog's Temperature

To measure your dog's temperature, use a pet thermometer. Pet stores now sell easy-to-use thermometers that are inserted into the dog's ear. If you're using a rectal thermometer, first shake the thermometer with a quick flick of your wrist until it reads less than 94° F. Then apply a small amount of petroleum jelly. Lift your dog's tail and slowly insert the thermometer approximately one inch into their rectum for two minutes. The normal temperature range for dogs is between 100° F and 102.5° F.

Handling Specific Medical Emergencies

This section describes how to treat identifiable medical

emergencies. Always perform the steps in the same order they're presented.

Bleeding

Bleeding can result from an accident, a fight with another animal, or from contact with a sharp object. These are generalized directions:

Apply direct pressure to the wound	Gently press a clean compress or cloth over the bleeding area; allowing it to clot. Keep adding more material or gauze as needed. If a section of bone is exposed or protruding from a wound – cover it with a bandage and apply gentle pressure.
Apply pressure to the artery supplying the blood	Apply pressure to the femoral artery (the groin area) for bleeding in the rear leg; the brachial artery (on the inside of the front leg) for front leg bleeding; and the caudal artery (at the inside base of the tail) for tail bleeding.
Elevate the point of bleeding	In addition to applying direct pressure, try to elevate the area that's bleeding.
Only apply a tourniquet as a last resort	Only use a tourniquet as a last resort since it can result in severe tissue damage or the loss of a limb. Be sure to loosen the tourniquet for 15 seconds every 10 minutes.

	Cleaning a wound should only be done by a vet. If you attempt to clean a wound, it could increase the likelihood of an infection.

Broken Bones

Broken bones are tricky because dogs often make matters worse by moving. If you suspect your dog has a broken bone, take these steps:

Muzzle your dog	Dog's with broken bones are usually in severe pain. Therefore, use a muzzle to prevent the possibility of someone (such as you) getting hurt.
Secure them any way you can	While keeping your dog as calm as possible, secure them to a padded object such as a board, a table top, or a ladder. Alternatively, wrap them in sheets, blankets, or clothing. Then secure them with rope, duct tape, or a belt.
Immobilize any broken limbs	Never attempt to set (straighten) a fracture. If a limb is broken; keep it still by wrapping it in gauze, clothing, or cotton padding. Then create a splint using a magazine, rolled up newspaper, towels, or two sticks. The splint should extend one joint above the fracture and one joint below. Secure the splint with

	tape but make sure that the tape doesn't constrict blood flow.
Immobilize your dog and get them to a vet	If your pet's spine, ribs, or hips appear injured or broken, gently place them on a stretcher and immobilize them any way you can. Never try to straighten a broken limb. Then get them to a vet.

 NEVER TRY TO SET A BROKEN LEG
The purpose of a splint it to immobilize the dog's broken bone, not to set it. Never try to set (straighten) a broken limb. This procedure must always be performed by an experienced vet with the assistance of an x-ray.

Burns

Severe burns should always be handled at a hospital. However, for minor burns, take the following steps:

Apply cool water	Run cool water over the affected area. If you're dealing with a chemical burn (like an acid), rinse the affected area with baking soda and water for at least 15 minutes. If necessary, use a mild soap and repeat until the area is thoroughly rinsed off.
Don't apply lotions	Topical ointments can spread burns. As a result, avoid the immediate use of

	ointments, petroleum jelly, or lotions.
Cover the burned area	Cover the burned area with a non-stick dressing to keep it clean. The dressing will also serve to prevent your dog from licking the area. Then, take your dog to a vet.

Car Accidents

If your dog has been hit by a car or involved in an accident, get them to a vet as quickly as possible. In the meantime, follow the procedures described here:

Get them to safety	The first priority is to make sure that you and your dog are safe. If you're near a road, move off to the side and find a way to make sure they can't run off!
Keep them calm	Place your dog in a crate, a box, or a vehicle. Then keep them quiet until you get to a vet.
Check for signs of shock	Your dog may be in shock. Symptoms may include weakness, collapse, unconsciousness, coolness of the skin, rapid but weak pulse, rapid respiration, staring eyes, dilated pupils, or pale lips, mouth, or eyelids.

Elevate your dog	Elevate your dog's chest above their head by placing folded towels under their rib cage and shoulders. This will help to increase blood flow to their brain while preventing fluids from filling their chest area.
Stop any bleeding	Examine your dog and treat any visible signs of bleeding (refer to the previous section).
Perform CPR if required	If your dog is unconscious, place them on their side with their head extended. Then follow the steps for CPR (described previously).
Keep them warm	Try to warm your dog using towels, blankets, or clothing. Don't give them any food or water at this time. Regardless of your dog's apparent condition, take them to a vet immediately.

Drowning

To treat a drowning dog, you'll have to administer CPR. However, you must first clear their airway and empty their lungs as described here:

Open their airway	Once your dog is on dry land, clear out their mouth, pull their tongue forward and extend their neck back to open their airway.

Drain their lungs of water	If your dog is small, suspend them by their hind legs and gently swing them to drain their lungs. For a larger dog, place him head down on a sloped surface, such as your outstretched legs.
Perform CPR	Check for breathing. If necessary, perform rescue breathing and CPR as described earlier in this chapter.

Exposure and Hypothermia

If you're looking for a lost dog, bring water, a blanket and a first aid kit. When you do find them, perform the following procedures:

Confirm their condition	Exposure and hypothermia are characterized by violent shaking and shivering followed by lethargy, listlessness and exhaustion.
Warm them up	Keep your dog warm with blankets, clothing, or anything else that you can find.
Monitor their temperature	Monitor your dog's temperature every ten to fifteen minutes. When their temperature is back to normal (between 100° F and 102.5° F), stop warming them. Pet stores now sell easy-to-use thermometers that are inserted into the

dog's ear. Even if your dog seems okay –
take them to the vet.

Gunshot Wounds

Gunshot wounds will vary depending on the type of
gun used and the severity of the wound. The procedures
described here must be implemented very quickly.

Cover the wound	Apply moistened gauze pads or clothing to the wound. If the pads become soaked in blood, don't remove them. Instead, keep adding more pads until the bleeding stops.
Apply pressure	Apply firm pressure to stop the bleeding. If the wound is to the chest area, press firmly to prevent air from getting into the dog's lungs. Use adhesive tape or stretch gauze to hold the padding in place.
Keep them calm	Keep your dog as calm as possible. If they move, it could make the injuries worse. Carefully secure them to a padded board, a table top, or a ladder. Alternatively, wrap them in sheets, blankets, or clothing. Use rope, duct tape, or a belt to hold them in place.
Get them to a vet	Your dog must be taken to a vet immediately. Tell the vet everything you know about the injury including the

gun's caliber, how far away he was from the gun when he was shot and the total number of shots. Then let the vet take over.

If possible, see what kind of ammo was used on your dog.

Dehydration and Heatstroke

Dehydration is normally caused by a dog being exposed to heat and dryness for an excessive period of time. If your dog appears listless and exhibits the characteristics of dehydration, do the following:

Test for dehydration	To test for dehydration, lift the skin along your dog's back. It should quickly spring back into place when you let go. If the skin stays up at all – your dog is probably dehydrated.

Wet them down	If your dog appears heat stressed (excessive panting, staggering, or shaking), take them to a shady location, and gently pour lukewarm water over their head and body. Symptoms of dehydration include dry mouth, sunken eyes, loss of elasticity in the skin, and extreme exhaustion.
Slowly give them water	Provide your dog with water, but don't allow them to gulp it down. This could result in severe vomiting and increased dehydration. Remove the bowl after a few sips and wait a couple of minutes before letting them take another drink. Without delay, seek veterinary care. Dehydration is a serious condition and must be treated immediately.

Electric Shock

Electrical shocks usually happen quickly and unexpectedly. The faster you can administer CPR, the better. Here's what to do:

Get them to safety	Make sure that your dog is no longer in contact with the power source. If they are, don't touch them. Move them with a wooden object. Then throw the switch or whatever you can to kill the power.

Perform CPR if required	Follow the steps for CPR described previously in this chapter. Then seek veterinary care. Shocks are serious and must be treated immediately.

Snake Bites

The key with snake bites is to keep your dog calm while getting them to an emergency care facility. If you already know where the nearest facility is, you are in good shape. If you don't, find out where one is right now (see box at beginning of chapter). Here's what to do if your dog gets bitten by a snake:

Make sure they've actually been bitten	If your dog has been bitten by a venomous snake, they will typically shake; drool; vomit; have dilated pupils; or collapse. They may also have swelling or bruising at the site of the bite. Never attempt to capture or kill the snake since this often results in more bites.
Keep them calm	If your dog has been bitten, it's crucial that you keep them calm. Don't let them walk, thrash about, or run. Just keep them as still as possible.
Don't treat them yourself	Avoid medications of any type; especially pain medications; cortisone; tranquilizers; or DMSO. Similarly, don't

	use ice, tourniquets, alcohol, or cut & suck techniques.
Get help fast	Get your dog to an emergency animal care facility as quickly as possible. Call ahead to give the clinician time to prepare the antivenin.

Poisons

If you think your dog might have been poisoned, follow these steps:

Confirm their condition	Suspect poisoning if your dog is having seizures; has trouble breathing; has severe diarrhea; has a slow or fast heartbeat; has burns around his mouth and lips; or is bleeding from the mouth or anus.

CALL THE ANIMAL POISON CONTROL CENTER AT 1-888-426-4435

The National Animal Poison Control Center has one of the largest databases in the world.
Consequently, they can provide you with crucial information and professional support over the phone.
Call them now!

Confirm their condition

Don't induce vomiting if the ingested substance is either unknown or caustic (it could make matters worse). Also, never induce vomiting if: your dog is having trouble breathing; is having seizures; has a bloated abdomen; or the label (of the ingested substance) explicitly says not to induce vomiting. On the other hand, always induce vomiting for these substances:

- Antifreeze
- Arsenic
- Aspirin
- Pesticides
- Kitchen Matches
- Medications
- Shampoo
- Shoe Polish
- Strychnine (rat poison)
- Warfarin (if just taken)

WAYS TO INDUCE VOMITING
(IN ORDER OF DESIRABILITY)

1. **Hydrogen Peroxide:** Give one teaspoon for every ten pounds of body weight. Wait fifteen minutes. If it doesn't work, repeat the dose.

2. **Dry Mustard:** Mix one teaspoon of dry mustard into one cup of lukewarm water. Administer slowly.

3. **Ipecac:** This works; but sometimes the dog will start vomiting and not be able to stop (making it the least desirable option).

A First Aid Kit for Dogs

This is a very comprehensive first-aid kit. You don't need one as complete as this. At a minimum, make sure that you have dressings and bandages for dressing a wound.

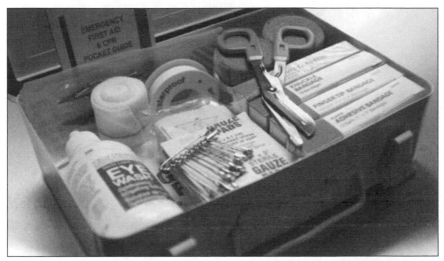

In a true emergency — even a very basic first-aid kit is a lot better than nothing.

A Complete First-Aid Kit for a Dog

TOOLS

- ❏ Scissors
- ❏ Needle Nose Pliers
- ❏ Forceps
- ❏ Toenail Clippers
- ❏ Surgical Gloves
- ❏ Thermometer

❑ Inflatable Splints

❑ Penlight

❑ Flea Comb

❑ Tweezers

DRESSINGS AND BANDAGES

❑ Roll of Flexible Bandage

❑ Non-stick Pads

❑ Roll of Adhesive Tape

❑ Towels

❑ Gauze Pads (4" x 2")

❑ Suturing Materials

❑ Cloth Strips

❑ Trauma Pads (6" x 9")

❑ Stretch Gauze

❑ Cotton Swabs

❑ Iodine Wipes

❑ Insect Wipes

TREATMENTS AND MEDICATIONS

❑ Benadryl

❑ Glucose Paste or Corn Syrup

❑ Enteric-Coated Aspirin

❑ Anti-Diarrhea Medicine

❑ Pepto-Bismol

❑ Eye and Ear Drops

❑ Oral Antibiotics

❑ Emetics (to induce vomiting)

❏ Pain Medications (aspirin)

❏ Hair Ball Ointment

❏ Sterile Eye Wash

❏ Epsom Salts

❏ Calamine Lotion

❏ Antibiotic Ointment

❏ Baking Soda (for stings)

❏ KY Jelly

❏ Petroleum Jelly

❏ Stop-Bleeding Powder

❏ Hydrocortisone Ointment

❏ 3% Hydrogen Peroxide

❏ Topical Antiseptic

❏ Rubbing Alcohol

❏ Skin Wash

Bosley the English Bull Dog, like most dogs, loves life on the road. Always make sure that you are prepared for a fun and safe journey *(courtesy of Derick Green)*.

Pet Health Record

Background Information	
Date:	
Name:	
Breed:	
Male/Female:	
Weight:	
Date of Birth:	
Neutered/Spayed:	
Veterinarian's Name:	
Clinic's Phone:	
License Tag #:	
Tag ID #:	
Microchip Company:	
Other:	

Vaccine	Immunization Dates						Veterinarian
Primary Vaccines: Normally administered at 1 to 3 year intervals							
Canine Distemper							
Canine Parvovirus							
Canine Adenovirus-2							
Rabies							
Secondary Vaccines: Normally administered on an as-needed basis							
Parainfluenza Virus							
Bordetella							
Lyme Disease							
Leptospirosis							

Special medical and/or dietary issues:

The information contained in this chapter is provided as a service to our readers. Neither the authors, Woodall's Publication Corp., its affiliates or agents, or any other party involved in the preparation or publication of the works presented here is responsible for any errors or omissions in information provided within this section or any other results obtained from the use of such information. Readers are encouraged to confirm the information contained herein with other reliable sources and to direct any questions concerning emergency pet care to licensed veterinarians or other appropriate pet health care professionals. While the authors and Woodall's Publication Corp. have endeavored to make sure the information contained in this site is accurate, we cannot guarantee the accuracy of such information and it is provided without warranty or guarantee of any kind. This book is not intended as a substitute for medical advice from a licensed veterinarian. The diagnosis and treatment of pet medical and emergency conditions depends upon a comprehensive history, physical examination, and a careful assessment of alternative treatment modalities, including the benefits, risks, and limitations of each. Woodall's Publication Corp. and the authors disclaim liability and are not legally responsible if the information provided is incomplete, inaccurate, or inapplicable to a reader's specific circumstances.

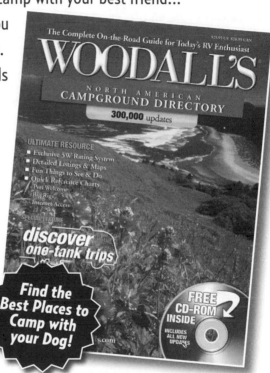

INDEX

B

C

D

R

S

T

U

V

W